Don't G n?!

How Progress, Not   **Life.**

seph

Be More Raw
Phoenix, AZ 85003

www.BeMoreRaw.com

Photo Credit:
Micheal Levack
Levack Photography

Cover:
Leeah Murray
Meraki & Co

This book is dedicated to my family for standing by me and supporting me emotionally and financially while I follow my dreams.

Dad, I'm so proud of the changes you've made. You are my favorite client.

Char, thank you for adopting a thirty-something year old and becoming at Grandma during your retirement.
We love you.

Mom, thank you so much for putting up with me while my son and I took over your house. I couldn't have done this without you.

Krystal. I will do my best to be there for your children and be a positive, healthy influence in their lives. I love you and miss you.

This book is also dedicated to my amazing son, who is the motivation for everything I do.

be more raw.

Organic Life Style

www.bemoreraw.com

FORWARD

Have you ever lost anyone to cancer? Do you know anyone with diabetes? These are just some of the chronic conditions that plague Americans today. Childhood diabetes, heart disease, and obesity have been steadily increasing over the past few decades. Along-side this constant growth in disease were significant changes to our food system. Additionally, our environmental issues are deteriorating and getting worse; global warming isn't getting any cooler.

Wait, global warming??? How can all these things be related? And how can any of these problems be solved? These are struggles that are too big for 1 person to do anything about. Right? By the end of this book you will see these seemingly impossible connections between issues with our home, Planet Earth, and the current health concerns that afflict Americans today, and increasingly the rest of the world.

Unlikely Vegan

I'm vegan. Yup. Hippie, granola, crunchy, whatever you want to call it; that's me (although I think I'm much more stylish than a pair of Birkenstocks and a hemp dress). Vegan means I don't eat anything that is or came from an animal. This also means that I don't wear or buy anything that supports the torture, killing, or enslavement of any animal. I don't wear leather. I don't use silk. I don't own furs or feathers. No grilled or sautéed animals, no butter, cheese milk or even Ghee. I never thought I'd end up here. I was your typical alpha-female. I would make obnoxious comments like, *"I love bacon!"* regularly. I would make jokes about killing animals for fun just for my enjoyment and taste. I've said (much like most vegans) I could never give up meat and definitely not cheese. Well, let me tell you something. No one gives up meat because of the way it tastes. I've never met a vegan that just stopped liking bacon one day. The decision to go vegan for me was gradual. It wasn't a particular moment in time that I can put my finger on and tell you when I decided I couldn't do it anymore.

So why did I decide to title this book *"Don't Go Vegan?!"* Look, I'm not here to tell you what to do. I'm here to educate, inform and **motivate** you. I am here to tell you the truth. The truth about health. The truth about animal agriculture. The truth about GMOs. But it's a journey. It's taken me YEARS to get to where I'm at. And I'm not perfect by any means. In fact, I don't believe in perfect. I believe in baby steps. I believe in taking control of your life. I believe in love, light and truth. This book is going to inform and enlighten you on these topics and explain how you can take small steps to better your well-being, reverse chronic illness, and improve the health of the planet at the same time.

How YOU feelin'?

You always hear people talking about "feeling better." I never knew what they were talking about. What does it feel like when you "feel better?" That's such a vague statement. Does it mean you wake up smiling and jumping out of bed? Or is it just the absence of feeling "bad?" No farting, no constipation, no stress, no flab. Is that what they mean by *"feeling better?"*

Maybe you're one of the many Americans that feels like crap. You're bloated, gassy, on three or more medications that have side effects that require more medication and you just don't feel like yourself. Maybe you're thinking, "Well, I don't feel so bad right now." You get up, go for walks and enjoy your wine. You eat, what you consider, a relatively balanced diet and you like to treat yourself when you go out. No matter which of these you relate to, I want to reveal how to not just "feel better," but how to feel your *best* and why.

I know most of us think pain, spider veins, disease, indigestion, aches and stiffness are synonymous with aging, but they are not. Yes, certain things do degrade with age and time, but not at the rate that we're used to. If we take care of our body by giving it what it needs, our body will take care of us. Aging doesn't have to be painful or miserable. Dr. Gabriel Cousens is 84 years old and practices yoga daily, is self sufficient, independent and active. He is just one example that ending up in a nursing home doesn't have to be your fate.

The human body is amazing. Because we are such impressive creatures, when we're young and in our 20s and 30s, we feel pretty immune and eat whatever we want. We rarely gain a pound or feel fatigued while pushing our bodies to the limit nutritionally. I look back at my years of eating Jack In The Box and Taco Bell, *multiple* times a day and wonder how I remained alive.

Even if you're over 40 or 50 years old and not feeling any effects from your diet and lifestyle choices (which is unlikely and rare), it's important to note the facts and the science behind eating too much meat and dairy **multiple times a day**.

The truth is, we (Americans) eat way too much meat. As you will see, meat is directly correlated and casually linked to cancer, diabetes and other chronic illness. We eat more meat than almost any other developed country and also have the highest disease and cancer rates. Coincidence? Maybe, maybe not.

Some might argue that we've been eating meat since the dawn of the century, but the fact of the matter is, that we were eating *mostly* raw fruits, veggies, nuts and seeds. The meat we consumed was far and few between fresh, raw organic produce. Not to mention, it wasn't full of hormones, antibiotics or genetically modified as is today's meat.

Why Plants?

There is an abundance of science, studies and research that points to the fact that **more** plant based, whole foods in one's diet will make for better health. From studies like the *Blue Zones* to research done by doctors like Dr. Gabriel Cousens and Dr. Caldwell Esselsytn, among others, the science has been making its way from the underground of anecdotal stories to mainstream media and into our living rooms. Many doctors like Dr. Nick Delgado, Garth Davis, and Brooke Goldner are actually ***prescribing*** a plant based diet to their patients. We deserve to give this a closer look.

During the 1920s H.P. Himsworth assembled existing research comparing plant based and animal based diets with rates of diabetes. As a plant based diet increases, diabetic deaths plunge from 20 to about 3 per 100,000 people. This is one of many studies that demonstrate the decrease in diabetes against a plant based diet.

James Anderson, M.D., studied these same principles under controlled environments. After three weeks the Type 1 diabetics were able to decrease their insulin medication by an average of 40%. The cholesterol levels of the patients dropped by 30%. That is astonishing, especially considering diabetics have two to four times more risk of stroke and of death from heart disease, and that over 70% of diabetics have high blood pressure. The Type 2 diabetics had even more impressive results. Over 95% of patients discontinued their medication after simply changing their diet. This was just one of many studies that prescribed a low-fat, plant based diet to diabetic patients in controlled environments with amazing results.

The China Study is a well known study conducted over a period of 20 years. The results of this study led to the publication of a book and the popular and widely acclaimed documentary, Forks Over Knives. It is widely renowned as one of the most comprehensive studies linking diet and disease **EVER**. Dr. Colin T. Campbell, a nutritional scientist, was one of the directors of this extensive study. The China Study looks at mortality rates in different regions of China and compares it to their consumption of animal products. It examines coronary heart disease, diabetes, and different cancers. An entire site, multiple books and eating programs have stemmed from the success of the documentary Forks Over Knives based on this study.

Forks Over Knives discusses how Dr. Esselsytn and Dr. Campbell had virtually the same discovery about the effects of animal protein (casein) hundreds of miles away. Dr Esselsytn was a successful heart surgeon. They both realized that many of the diseases that were common in America were virtually unknown in different parts of the world where the diet is more plant based. This lead them to conduct their own studies separately before joining forces later to compile their accumulative research. The most revealing small scale study Dr. Campbell conducted was on mice. He fed the animals casein and found as he increased the consumption it would increase their tumor and cancer growth. As he decreased the consumption of casein the cancer would disappear. This is important because he realized that we could essentially turn cancer off and on. Although genetics may play a part in us being more prone to certain diseases, *"diet pulls the trigger."*

Dr. Michael Greger is an established medical doctor who not only preaches to eat a plant based diet but also practices one himself for over 20 years and has written four books. His most famous publication, *How to Not Die*, made the New York Times best seller list three times. I like and trust Dr. Greger's work because he establishes his claims through sound, evidence-based research compiled across life spans. He remains unbiased and factual with the information he provides.

Dr. Brooke Goldner is another doctor with impressive credentials that has discovered the power of plants. Dr. Goldner graduated with honors from Carneige Mellon University and received her MD from Temple University School Of Medicine. She was the Medical Director of the Transition Age Youth Academy and The Wellness Center for Mental Health America. She completed revolutionary genetic research in Leukemia, neurobiology and is certified in Plant-Based Nutrition from Cornell University. She has been featured in *Vegan Health and Fitness Magazine* multiple times.

Brooke was diagnosed with Lupus and stage IV kidney disease at 16 years old. She was told she would never be able to have children. Creating her very own protocol using common plant based foods from the grocery store, she healed herself from Lupus at 28 years old. She then went on to prove the medical world wrong and had two healthy, vegan pregnancies and children. Her article in *Vegan Health and Fitness Magazine* helped me, specifically, during my pregnancy.

Dr. Garth Davis is a weight loss expert and surgeon. Dr. Davis claims he is a "new" athlete because most of his life he wasn't an athlete at all. The short biography on his site reveals how he was "lazy" and a "bum" most of his life. As a gastric bypass surgeon, his former patients motivated him to learn more about the connection between diet and disease. He admits that Medical Doctors (M.D.s not to be confused with N.D.s) only receive about **one hour** of nutritional education in school. The Blue Zones details a concept by National Geographic in which they studied five specific parts of the world where the majority of people's life expectancy are near or over 100 years old. These people aren't just *barely* living to be 100. They are still very present, cognitive, independent and active. Ikaria, Greece, Nicoya Peninsula in Costa Rica, Okinawa, Japan and the Barbagia region of Sardinia all have life expectancies around the age of 100 years old. They found that these five parts of the world have nine things in common.

Two of these nine traits are food related. One of the characteristics says to stop eating when 80% full which helps prevent over-eating. The other thing they all have in common is that whole plants are the cornerstone of their diet. *If* they eat meat at all, it is few and far between, somewhere around only **five times per month.**

I met Dr. Nick Delgado a few years back at *The Raw Living Expo* (renamed *Pure Joy Expo*). He is not only a vegan but is a world record holding body builder. In his 50s he competes with 30 year olds and **wins**. He healed his child's autism without medication and has over 50,000 MD followers on his site promoting natural medicine and plant based nutrition to the public and MDs around the nation.

Eggs Can't Be THAT Bad

The incredible edible egg: full of cholesterol and dioxin (yes, even your organic, grass fed, eggs). Eggs are the number one source of dietary cholesterol in the American diet. According to the latest meta-analysis (an analysis and compilation of multiple studies) going back all the way to 1930, eggs have a severely negative effect on health. This meta-analysis covers dozens of studies covering hundreds of study subjects. Persons that consumed the most eggs had an increased risk of cardiovascular disease by 19% and a 68% increased risk of diabetes. Once an individual has diabetes, their risk for heart disease increases by 85%. The amount of egg consumption needed to acquire these results may surprise you. **Less than one single egg per day** was associated with a notably increased risk for heart disease. Consuming anything over half of one egg per day increases the risk for diabetes by 29%.

What about egg whites? Those are healthier, right? They do lack all the cholesterol that's packed in that egg yolk, but they still come with dioxin among other things

(Don't worry; we'll get to the fun of dioxin later on). Eggs are a great way to get parasites as they are one of the most bacteria laden foods in our food system. Salmonella is found naturally in chicken intestines regardless of how the chicken is raised. Just upon cracking open your organic or factory farmed egg, you're exposed to salmonella and other unsafe bacterias. Although cooking does destroy bacteria, it will remain on your hands, even after washing. Salmonella can only be destroyed if the cooking time is *long enough* and the *heat is high enough.* So that over easy, runny egg may still have some present. Salmonella food poisoning symptoms include fever, nausea, dehydration, abdominal pain, cramping and headache that can last up to a week.

Biotin, aka B7, or lack thereof, is another reason why egg-whites are **not a health food.** Besides the more common known beauty benefits of this special B vitamin including nice hair, skin and nails, it's crucial for healthy digestion, metabolism and brain function. All B vitamins are important for optimal brain health. Egg whites actually deplete the body's B7. Biotin deficiency can cause hair loss, seizure, lack of muscle tone, cramps and more.

Oats, mushroom, avocados, Swiss chard, sunflower seeds, peanut butter, cauliflower, berries, almonds, banana, chia, tomatoes, and onions are all good sources of B7.

100% vegan creations by Jayce Lab

Fish Are Healthy Though...Right?

Common knowledge tells us to consume fish for our Omegas 3s. But Dr. Greger, among other doctors, will tell you differently. When we eat fish, we're getting a lot more than just those sought after Omega 3s. Fish contain *many contaminants*. In one of my favorite videos of his entitled *"40 Year Vegan Dies of Heart Attack"* Dr. Greger outlines the importance of Omegas, B12, and Vitamin D. The video is years old and even **then** he lists the many toxins found in fish and unfortunately that amount has grown significantly.

Today fish are found containing multiple types of pharmaceuticals, PCBs, DDT, dioxins and we've all heard about mercury. Isn't it weird that pregnant women are told not to eat fish because of the mercury content but we've all been consuming it knowing that? These toxins are linked to cancer, neurological disorders, birth defects, and even thyroid problems. They are among the literally **most toxic known substances on the planet.**

Polychlorinated biphenyls (PCBs) are synthetic chemicals created for industrial purposes such as lubricants, plasticizers and commonly used in electrical equipment. PCBs affect thyroid and hormonal function, have been linked to a variety of cancers, and cause significant neurological and motor control problems in new borns.

DDT, or **dichlorodiphenyltrichloroethane and Agent Orange,** is a man-made chemical used in WWII to kill off the jungle for troops to see and travel easier. DDT is linked to premature births, low birth weight, and effects on liver and reproduction. It is considered a probably human carcinogen.

Radiation has recently become an *additional* concern with wild caught seafood found in the pacific. Although the Fukishima nuclear plant disaster happened in 2011, there have been reports in 2013, 2015 and 2016 of fish (including Cod, Halibut, Tuna, and Sea Bass to name a few) with dangerously high levels of radiation. According to reports made by Superstation95 fish are getting cancer, tumors, deformities and even Alopecia (hair loss). There are graphic photos of bloodied tumorous salmon, shrimp, shark, and other wild animals suffering from radiation damage on their site.

Consuming fish pose especially dangerous for pregnant women. According to *Tufts University Health and Nutrition Letter,* pregnant women who ate fish from Lake Michigan reported babies that displayed abnormal reflexes, general weakness, slower responses to external stimuli and signs of depression. It was also noted that women that ate fish only a **couple times a month** created babies that weighed 7-9 ounces less at birth and had smaller heads. In a four year follow up study it was found that those children were not only associated with lower weights, but that short-term memory and their overall cognitive processing speed was lower.

If you're eating farmed fish, you're not safe either. Most of the farmed fish consumed in the US are commonly fed pig and chicken feces. Additionally, they are fed GMO feed of corn and soy which cause problems because it's not their natural diet. The GMO feed causes it's own additional problems which are discussed further in a later chapter. Just remember: *you are what you eat ate!* So if you're eating fish that ate GMOs, you're eating GMOs, too. If you're eating fish loaded with toxins, you're eating toxins, too!

Go Fish.
(without hurting any sea animals)

VeganStreet.com

Meat Ain't So Sweet

What causes blood sugar spikes and diabetes? Sugar, right? Well, that's what we've been taught. But evidence is telling us something different. Although sugar does affect our insulin levels, pancreas and blood sugar, what might be a more aggressive cause of diabetes appears to have more to do with fat and toxins than sugar.

According to the Clinical Nutrition Research Centre, meals mainly consisting of meat and dairy lead to exasperated spikes in sugar and fat in the blood. Meals like this create free radicals, which is like having a **sun burn on the inside of your body;** not good. Additionally, oxidative stress elicits a chain reaction in our circulation, damaging proteins in our body, inducing inflammation, paralyzing artery function, thickening our blood, and causing a fight-or-flight nerve response. All of this occurs within **less than 4 hours** of eating a meal. This means that just one poor breakfast decision could have a crippling effect on your health.

Most Americans are eating this way multiple times a day. This way of living is a significant contributor to heart disease. However, your typical doctor, who **isn't**

trained in nutrition, measures your blood sugar and fat levels in a fasting state, meaning taking your blood *before* you've eaten. So if you've had blood work done and think you're safe or healthy, think again. What happens *after* a meal seems to be a stronger predictor of heart attacks and strokes.

Another study observed non-diabetic women with heart disease, but normal fasting blood sugar. It revealed that how high their blood sugar spikes after consuming sugar water seems to determine how fast their arteries continue to clog up. Dr. Micheal Greger reviewed this data and hypothesized that this might occur because the higher the blood sugar spike, the more free radicals are produced. A *whole food, plant based* diet in antioxidant, anti-inflammatory foods has shown to **eliminate** the after-meal increase in sugar, fat and inflammation.

An interesting note is what happens when comparing *low carb animal foods and low carb plant based* foods. If you consumed a slice of white bread your blood sugar would spike within an hour. However, if you consumed that same bread with plant based fats and proteins (like almond butter or nuts) the blood sugar spike significantly reduces. One study measured the blood sugar spike after combining the healthiest form of cooking meat, a steamed skinless chicken breast, with white rice. The insulin spike was much greater than consuming the white rice alone. The results were the same when tested with animal fat. As butter was added to a meal, the insulin spike was significantly higher. When adding two sources of animal fat and protein of butter and cheese to a "white" product (bread, potatoes, pasta, rice, etc.) the insulin spike would double in some cases. But once again, after adding a plant source of fat or protein like avocado, the insulin response improves.

How interesting that adding the plant based fat and protein made things better, but adding the animal fat and protein food made things considerably worse. *Why is this?* The antioxidants found **only in plant foods** have the ability to **eliminate** free radicals. Only nourishing, whole food, *plant based* fats and protein like nuts, can dampen blood sugar spikes, cripple oxidative damage and lower insulin spikes.

Here's the thing about cholesterol, our body actually **makes** cholesterol. We don't need to eat it. The only kind of cholesterol that can clog our arteries is called dietary cholesterol which is found **only in animal foods**. Chicken, pork, beef, butter, dairy, eggs, and yes, even fish contain cholesterol. A fatty piece of salmon can have as much cholesterol as a pork chop.

You don't really want to eat her, do you?

Photo by Laura Anderson

The Colon Whisperer

I was constipated throughout most of my 20s and had hemorrhoids frequently. Like most Americans, I didn't really think anything of it, and thought having a bowel movement a few times a week was "normal." Many MDs, today, will still tell you that bowel frequency varies from person to person. **This is not true.** Just like every species' diet, there is a biological norm. We are supposed to have one bowel movement for every meal we eat.

Tummy, gut, GI, colon, stomach, intestines. Whatever you want to call it, its impact, influence and importance in our overall health is significantly underrated. Over 70% of our immune system is in our colon and new evidence is showing an immense connection between brain health and colon health. Keeping it functioning properly affects other organs, blood, cognition and therefore our whole body and whole-body health.

The colon is one of our core systems to detoxify, cleanse and heal. The intestinal walls are moist and tightly bound, or at least they should be. When we eat dead, processed foods and take pharmaceuticals and antibiotics it disrupts our gut flora and kills off good bacteria. These good bacteria are responsible for digestion, immune function and keeping our colon working properly.

During the digestion process, food is consumed and broken down to its individual property, such as protein and carbohydrate. Anything larger than this the body doesn't recognize and therefore treats as a toxin. When our digestive wall becomes porous due to poor diet and toxic medications, things are able to pass through the colon wall in large pieces. As a result, the colon becomes inflamed.

It literally takes DAYS to digest meat. When food, *any food,* sits in our colon it begins to **putrefy and rot**. This creates gaseous by-products and irritate the colon which leads to inflammation and can contribute to leaky gut. So, if you're eating meat at all, it shouldn't be more than 1-2 times per week. We're eating it for breakfast, lunch and dinner! The average male has about 5 pounds of undigested red meat in his colon at any given time. It wreaks havoc on the digestion, assimilation and immune systems.

There are two types of food allergies: Immunoglobulin E (IgE) and Immunoglobulin G (IgG).

IgE is the anaphylactic shock kind that we're all familiar with. These are called IgE. You know, the guy that can't touch a peanut or he'll need an epi pen. IgG is more subtle. IgE measures the blood levels of these particular antibodies. Our immune system makes antibodies to attack any foreign invaders like antigens, viruses, bacteria and allergens. Immunoglobulin G (IgG) are antibodies that provides longer resistance to infections or foreign invaders.

IgG allergens are often not recognized in the traditional western medicine and you may have to see a Naturopathic Doctor (ND) to get this test. These types of allergens manifest as much more subtle symptoms than the immediate symptoms of IgE. When our colon is porous and there are large pieces of food floating around in our bloodstream where they don't belong, our body triggers this protection mechanism. This is how certain food allergies can be formed.

Many people live with IgG food allergies for years and sometimes their entire lives. One reason for this is because most of the mainstream medical community doesn't recognize it. Another reason is because the symptoms are not only subtler, but not always immediate.

Symptoms can manifest anywhere from *hours to days after* the food has been consumed. Headache and nausea to seizure and hyperactivity, or simply just fatigue, bloating, mood changes or dark circles under the eyes are all possible symptoms. The length and severity of the symptoms are completely dependent of the person.

Dr. David Perlmutter, a well respected neurologist discovered a stunning link between Alzheimer's and brain health and gut health. When the permeability of the colon is such that food particles *or pharmaceuticals* are able to cross that barrier, it challenges our immune system and sets off a "cascade" of inflammation affecting everything including your immune system and even brain health.

Cleansing the colon is an incredibly effective, and natural way to clean out all that sh*t! Excuse my language, but it's true. Due to pharmaceuticals, antibiotics, processed and dead foods, most of our colons aren't in the best shape, literally. Some of us have prolapsed colons, IBS or colitis. We go to the doctor and they give us a completely synthetic and toxic pill to remedy our symptoms but tell us nothing about what to eat or do to fix the **root issue.** Colon cleansing allows the old, hardened matter to soften and then release. Only then, can we begin to heal the colon and restore its integrity.

Some form of colon irrigation has been used regularly as far back as Egyptian times in the 14th century (Those clever Egyptians!). The Egyptians believed in the very early concept of *auto-intoxication*. This belief stated that after years of food being in the body, it decomposes then moves into the circulatory system therefore causing maladies and sickness of many kinds.

Centuries later, the benefits and methods of colon irrigation continued to improve and frequent. Europeans commonly used enemas to promote overall health and successfully heal fever, anxiety and illness. Through the 17th and 19th century it was still practiced and advanced. During the 17th century it was common practice in the Parisian culture to have 3-4 enemas a day believing that internal cleansing was the path to well-being. Towards the end of the 19th century colon irrigation equipment improved and allowed colon cleansing to be extended to the large intestine.

James A. Wiltsie M.D., Joseph Waddington M.D., and John H. Kellogg M.D. are some doctors in the 19th century that supported and perpetuated research of colon hydrotherapy. As published in the Journal of American

Medical Association (JAMA), Dr. John H. Kellogg reported using colon hydrotherapy in over 40,000 patients with gastrointestinal disease and using surgery in only 20 cases. To quote Dr. Waddington, in his work *"Scientific Intestinal Irrigation and Adjuvant Therapy"*, ***"Abnormal functioning of the intestinal canal is the precursor of much ill-health, especially of chronic disease."*** Dr. Wiltsie said, *"As long as we continue to assume the colon will take care of itself, it's just that long that we will remain in complete ignorance of perhaps the most important source of ill health in the whole body."*

Our bodies will adapt to whatever we put into it until it can't. For our colons, this means if we feed it lots of **dead, processed foods, meat and dairy**, it will become constipated, inflamed and for many, literally misshapen and stretched out. When you see someone, who isn't necessarily overweight but they have a huge beer belly, that usually means their colon is stretched out. A prolapsed colon is just one of many conditions that can manifest when we aren't good to our colons. For men, this pressure can mean excess back pain among, constipation and fatigue. For women, a prolapsed colon can mean heavier menstrual cramps in addition to pain and fatigue. Constipation, Irritable Bowel Syndrome, Diverticulitis, Leaky Gut, Colitis, Chron's Disease, and Colon Cancer are all symptoms of a prolapsed, weak, and degenerated colon.

One way our bodies adapt and protect us is by secreting a substance called **mucoid plaque.** This is expelled when we put anything into our bodies that the brain considers poison. Coffee, alcohol, sugar (unless it's pure, natural cane sugar) are all considered poisons by the brain. The plaque builds up and hardens into a plastic like substance coating our intestines. This affects our ability to absorb any healthy foods we might be putting into our bodies. The only way to get rid of this plaque is cleanse the colon.

Our colons didn't get misshapen and distressed overnight. It took years and years for waste to compile and porous holes to accumulate. It's naive of us to think that one or two sessions of colon hydrotherapy can remove all this waste. The industry standard recommends at least 3 back to back (3 days in a row) to get significant results. Most people need somewhere between 10-20 to get back to baseline. *Then the healing can begin.* When I first started my colon cleansing journey I had around 30 in a period of a few months. I've since had many more.

I consider the bowel movements of *every* client I work with. They tell me so much about what is going in inside the body. A truly healthy bowel movement will pass easily and be approximately the width of your wrist and the length from your wrist to your elbow. Now, don't get dsicouraged if yours is far from that. It took me *years* to have healthy bowel movements. Just take it one step at a time. Following my **5 simple steps** in this book will help lead you towards poops you can be proud of!

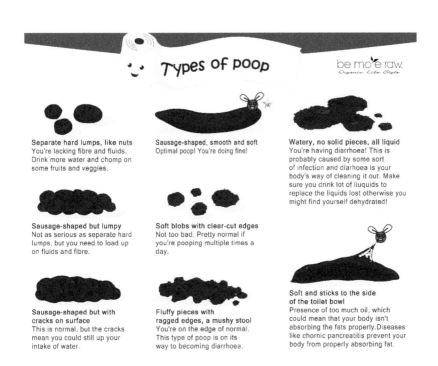

Types of poop

be mo'e raw.
Organic Life Style

Separate hard lumps, like nuts
You're lacking fibre and fluids. Drink more water and chomp on some fruits and veggies.

Sausage-shaped but lumpy
Not as serious as separate hard lumps, but you need to load up on fluids and fibre.

Sausage-shaped but with cracks on surface
This is normal, but the cracks mean you could still up your intake of water.

Sausage-shaped, smooth and soft
Optimal poop! You're doing fine!

Soft blobs with clear-cut edges
Not too bad. Pretty normal if you're pooping multiple times a day.

Fluffy pieces with ragged edges, a mushy stool
You're on the edge of normal. This type of poop is on its way to becoming diarrhoea.

Watery, no solid pieces, all liquid
You're having diarrhoea! This is probably caused by some sort of infection and diarrhoea is your body's way of cleaning it out. Make sure you drink lot of liuquids to replace the liquids lost otherwise you might find yourself dehydrated!

Soft and sticks to the side of the toilet bowl
Presence of too much oil, which could mean that your body isn't absorbing the fats properly.Diseases like chornic pancreatitis prevent your body from properly absorbing fat.

Is there a right and a wrong way to poop? Let's not think about what's right and wrong. I prefer optimal and less effective. Evolutionarily, we were designed to comfortably empty our bowels in one particular position. This position is squatting. As you can see by the image below, it relieves pressure by the puborectalis muscle, allowing bowels to fully empty with less strain.

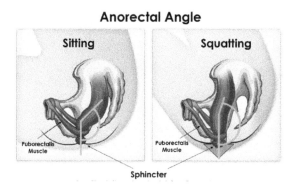

Anorectal Angle

I recommend **everyone** poop this way. You do not have to squat on your toilet to achieve this. You can purchase a *Squatty Potty* for around $20 on my site. But hell, I don't care if you use your toddler's step stool! The point is, we're straightening out those muscles so the bowels have no strain and can completely empty much more easily.

Pushing really hard while your going to the restroom (#2, that is) may also be considered normal. This inflicts extreme stress on your rectal muscles and causes hemorrhoids. Teach your children at an early age to breathe and take their time when going to the restroom. If it's taking you a really long time to pass your bowels, your body wants change!

Being a colon hydro-therapist has allowed me to cross paths and help those who are really sick and in need. I had a client that was on her death bed and very sick in the hospital. She eventually decided to try natural modalities and came to the center where I practice. Her mother was very "vocal" to say the least and not necessarily cooperative with the other therapists. I'm not sure what happened, but my approach was quiet, calm and sensitive, especially for those that are very senile, sick and apprehensive. From then on she would only have colonics if I was there. Her daughter nicknamed me,

"The Colon Whisperer."

Raw Power

Being a raw chef and enthusiast, I will always talk about the importance of raw food. However, in spite of what people think, I don't automatically put all my clients on a raw food diet. Although I will always include some raw foods, it is completely based on each individual case, but the healing power and basic benefits of raw foods deserves some attention.

Cooked and raw foods are a world apart. When we cook our food (plants or animal based), we're cooking off *50% protein, 60-80% of the vitamins and minerals and up to 95-100% of the phytonutrients.* **All of the enzymes** that help us digest our foods are destroyed. Additionally, when we eat cooked food it generates an immediate white blood cell count. This means when we eat cooked food our body is treating it like an invader to some extent.

Kirlian photography gives us another great example of the power of raw foods (and organic vs conventional!). Kirlian photography is named after Semyon Kirlian, who in 1939 accidentally discovered objects on the photographic plate with strong electric fields leave an imprint on the image on the plate. The thought behind the use of this photography with food, is that is reveals the aura, or **"life force"** of food. We know food gives us energy and nutrients, but taking another different perspective is that it gives us life, life force and energy. When cooked food and raw food is compared using Kirlian photography, you can clearly see the energy field difference between the two. You can also see the difference when comparing conventional food treated with pesticides and chemicals vs organic food.

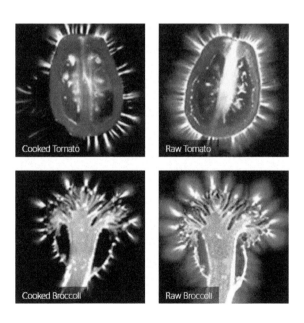

Water and fiber is what helps us "go." When we eat cooked food, it takes moisture from our colon to digest it. Whole, raw, plant based foods have all the water intact and help us stay regular. Fiber, by definition, is *only found in plants*. Meat and animal flesh contain NO FIBER.

We are all born with a reserve of enzymes. These enzymes were intended to digest food that was cooked in the rare event we didn't have raw food with it. Every time we put anything in our mouth, our brain recognizes it for what it is. When we put raw food in our mouth, our brain says, *"This is raw, it has all the enzymes necessary to digest it."* When cooked food enters our mouth, it pulls from our reserve of enzymes depleting them. Because most of us didn't grow up on raw fruits and vegetables, we used up all our enzymes. I don't know about you, but I grew up on hot dogs and pop-tarts. I don't even think my first food as a baby was raw. My mom said one of my first foods was mashed potatoes with butter and sugar (ech!).

Juicing has amazing healing benefits. A juice is a fruit and/or vegetable drink with the fiber removed and the liquid contained. You might be thinking, "Wait, don't we need fiber?" Yes, we do. But juicing offers marvelous gain with little effort from the body, literally.

When the fiber is removed from the fruit or vegetable, it is now a liquid. Our digestion doesn't have to work *at all* to absorb it. The effect is getting the most whole food nutrition absorbed the quickest way possible. The results can be **miraculous**.

Dr. Max Gerson among other doctors used organic, raw juices to heal cancer even its latest, terminal stages. Dr. Gerson was the most published doctors in the world until the United States Government and Medical Industry officially **banned him** from publishing his work. Publishing his works of success could have easily eradicated the medical and pharmaceutical industry as we know it.

He successfully healed *advanced* stages of cancer, acne, addictions, AIDS, allergies, anemias, ankylosing spondylitis, arthritis, asthma, cancer, candidiasis, chemical sensitivities, chronic fatigue, constipation, crohns disease, cushings syndrome,depression/panic attacks, diabetes, emphysema, endometriosis, epilepsy, fibromyalgia, fibroids, genital herpes, gout, heart and artery diseases, hemorrhoids, hepatitis, high blood pressure, hyperactivity, hypoglycemia/hyperglycemia, infertility, intestinal parasites, kidney Disease, Liver Cirrhosis, Lyme Disease, Lupus, Erythematosus,

Migraines, Macular Degeneration, mononucleosis, multiple sclerosis, obesity, ocular histoplasmosis, osteomyelitis, osteoporosis phlebitis (Varicose Veins), psoriasis, premenstrual syndrome, shingles, stroke, tuberculosis and ulcerative Colitis.

In the 1930s the scientist, Max Gerson, suffered from debilitating migraines. After going to the medical community and being offered no solution, he took matters into his own hands. He dramatically changed his diet removing meat, processed and fatty foods and replacing them with **organic, uncooked fruits and vegetables.** Within weeks his migraines had disappeared. Dr. Gerson began applying his new "migraine diet" to his patients and one of them came back to him cured. At this point he and a world-renowned surgeon, Ferdinand Sauerbruch, decided to study this in a controlled environment. They applied the diet to 460 tuberculosis patients and 456 of them were cured completely. This was the beginning of over 100 years of successful reversals and cures of so-called terminally ill patients.

The programs implemented here at *Be More Raw*, draw on Dr. Max Gerson's work along with other raw food pioneers including Dr. Gabriel Cousens. I was fortunate enough to work at Dr. Cousens' center for a month and got to experience first hand the amazing food and spirituality his center offers. If you can afford to go there, I highly recommend it. But those who can't afford over $12,000, my programs are a fraction of the cost with the same benefits and application. I work with clients one on one. I don't want you to just heal, but become educated and motivated to make a **permanent lifestyle change** you are excited about. I have personally worked with multiple clients that have healed their cancers and other ailments using my recommended modalities.

be more raw.
Organic Life Style

Sticks And Stems?

What is "raw food?" Sure sounds like sticks and stems to me. Ok, so we've defined what raw food is and why it's beneficial, but does that mean salads and smoothies are the only way to get there? **NO.**

There is an entire raw food community, including chefs like myself, coming up with creative and fantastic ways to mimic our favorite cooked dishes. This includes all the greats like lasagna, burgers, pizza and more.

When I say "raw bread," it's not uncooked flour and yeast. That would be gross! Raw bread, pizza, etc. is about using whole foods, usually nuts, seeds, vegetables, oils, spices, blended and assembled in a way that imitates those very foods.

Raw food has come a long way since the likes of Dr. Max Gerson who just knew of organic juices and simple dishes to achieve a raw food diet. *Hippocrates Health Institute, The Tree of Life* and *An Oasis of Healing* are all centers along with *Be More Raw,* that use elegant and sophisticated raw food meals (and juices) to heal and reverse chronic diseases.

There are a few examples of raw recipes in the back of this book. Follow *Be More Raw* on Instagram and Facebook to enjoy even more free recipes and inspiring dishes.

This is stressing me out.

What we put into our bodies goes so much deeper than our stomachs. It affects our moods, our emotions and our spirituality. When we are in a good mood or bad mood it can affect how we treat other people; people we care about or the person in line ahead of you. It can mean the difference between snapping at your bagger at the grocery store and a smile and pleasant conversation.

Did you know that what you feel actually affects the chemical reactions in your body? The body **needs** stress. It's actually good for us in small amounts. It serves a purpose in small amounts. It can help boost immunity and even brain power, but too much stress at the wrong times can be damaging and hindering to other processes.

In cavemen times if we were stressed it meant we were running from a wild animal trying to survive. When you are stressed or upset, your body is in fight or flight mode. Today it might mean your boss is getting on your nerves. Well, your body doesn't know the difference between a predator and your boss. It just knows what it needs to do.

When your body is in fight or flight mode, it's focusing on survival. Other processes in the body become a lower priority and/or shut down **completely**. Digestion is one of those processes. If you're angry, stressed or eating on the go at work, it can and will slow down and hinder your digestion making it harder to assimilate all those delicious, healthy foods you're about to eat.

Since 70-80% of our immune system is in our gut, it makes sense that taking care of yourself will help you take care of others. But a little known fact is that about 90% of our serotonin production is in our gut, too. This is why comfort food is comfort food; it makes us FEEL good! But good, healthy foods will have an even greater affect on our mood, mental clarity and temperament.

How can my personal health affect the ones I love? I, like most of you, have personally experienced this one too many times. I've been in a place where I wasn't taking good care of myself and therefore wasn't my best self. If I'm not getting enough sleep and not eating balanced meals, I become snappy, less patient and generally not happy.

Think about it, if you're in pain all the time, or uncomfortable because you're bloated or gassy, it's going to be a lot harder to muster up the patience for things going wrong during your day. My "cup" was empty, so to speak. I was less productive, I had WAY less patience, and got extra cranky. Something I also notice is I make food choices that aren't optimal. They're made out of haste and convenience.

I've also been on the receiving end of this stick. Living with my mom was challenging because she was stressed ALL THE TIME. She rarely got enough sleep and was addicted (like most of us) to sugar. I noticed that it directly affected our relationship because she would be rude, argumentative, spacey and just not herself at times.

Food affects your spirituality in more ways than one. Spirituality and science are one in the same. You see,

everything has a vibration *(that's science!).* Certain things vibrate higher and certain things lower. When you eat cooked, processed or dead food, it's vibrating low. Although blessing can raise the vibration of foods, it's harder to raise the vibration of something really low like a bag of Doritos than it is to raise something that's vibrating at a moderate or high level like raw, living, organic foods.

Vibrations are energy. So when you consume food, you're consuming energy in a number of ways. You're consuming the vibration level and also everything that came before it and anything that contributed to its being. Let me explain. Take a pig for example. I know a lot of us would like to think that when we get grass fed, pasture raised, free roaming "pork," it's a super happy life the pig lives until it comes to it's **bloody, slaughter**. But the fact of the matter is, if you're getting it from a grocery store, I don't care how expensive and what kind of label is on that pork, it experienced a gory, agonizing death. You're consuming all the energy, vibration and pain that animal went through.

If for some reason you *don't* believe in any of that "fru fru" stuff, we can look at physiology. Animals in factory farms are subjected to mental and emotional torture including constant loud noises, lack of or low quality sleep and physical abuse. Just like when we are in a stressful situation, certain chemical reactions happen in the body. Hormones are released, muscles tighten and change. Similar actions happen to an animal when they are scared, or stressed. Just before an animal is slaughtered hormones and toxic substances are released into their bodies that significantly alter and deteriorate the "meat." Their pH levels rise which causes discoloration in the meat (flesh). Adrenaline is released which uses up the body's glycogen. This will cause the animal's flesh to be tough, high in pH, tasteless and will actually spoil more quickly.

This is possibly why it is common practice to dye meats brighter red. These hormones and physical changes in the animal have negative affects on our health. Fatigue, impotence, high blood pressure and high cholesterol, diabetes and colon diseases are all associated with eating low quality and "stressed out" animal flesh.

Nutrients Discussed As A Vegan

Omegas

Omega 3s are important to the function of our immune, emotional, cognitive and hormonal systems and reduces overall inflammation in the body. Omegas are built of ALA, DHA and EPA. Omega 3s are strongly linked with a reduction and prevention in diseases of all kinds from heart diseases and cancer to diabetes and even arthritis. Low levels omega 3s have been associated with depression, lack of ability to concentrate or deal with stress and even suicide. Adequate omega 3s will protect against 80% of heart disease, great concentration, better and more stable moods, emotions and overall better health and brain function.

The most concentrated plant source of omegas 3 on planet is flax. Flax and walnuts have omegas in the form of ALA. Our bodies have work a little harder to convert this to the precious DHA and EPA that our bodies need. Dr. Cousens discovered that by combining your consumption of ground flax seed with 1-3 tablespoons of coconut oil the conversion rate is doubled. Fish's fatty flesh directly contain the fatty acids in the form of DHA and EPA, but hopefully after reading the dangers of consuming farm raised or wild caught fish, you'll want another source for your omega 3s.

According to Dean Ornish, MD, going to the source for Omegas is the best choice. When we eat fish, just like protein within chicken, the Omegas we get are recycled. They come from the sea plankton and algae the **fish ate.** Bypass the dead fish and go straight to the source: ALGAE.

Protein

Protein deficiency is a very real and serious condition. People who don't eat animal flesh and animal by-products run a dangerously high probability of being protein deficient.

JUST KIDDING!

There is absolutely NO DOCUMENTED CASE OF PROTEIN DEFICIENCY IN AMERICA! Do you know what protein deficiency looks like? It looks like those very sad children on infomercials you see to "feed a child on one dollar a day" with protruding bellies. They're not getting enough calories. The only way you run the risk of being protein deficient is if you're not eating enough calories. **Less than 3%** of Americans are not getting enough protein because of calorie restricted diets. But seriously, protein is very important. It's vital for our muscle and tissue repair, bones and cartilage. Protein is used to make enzymes and hormones aiding in digestion and stabilizing our moods. It also supports our neurological function.

Lucky for us protein is SUPER, DUPER ABUNDANT in plant foods! According to the *largest study in history* comparing plant based diets to pescatarians and vegetarians of over **70,000** participants, vegans and non-vegans all get about 70% more protein than needed. The recommended amount of protein is about 40 grams per day. About 97% of Americans are getting not only enough protein, but more than enough protein.

Too much protein is actually more of a problem. Your body can actually only use so much protein at a time. If you eat more than required your body simply converts it to sugar and then fat. These increased blood sugar levels contribute to diabetes, cancer cell growth and Candida. Excess protein is also strenuous on the liver and kidneys. When protein is consumed the liver breaks down the amino acids and nitrogen and ammonia forms during this process. The liver is responsible for filtering out the ammonia and your kidneys filter out nitrogen. When we consume too much animal protein (like *most of us* for breakfast lunch *and* dinner) the liver gets overworked and tired. This leads to a toxic environment in your body. Your colon and your kidneys start to lag and fail. Chronic dehydration, fatigue, strong and frequent urination, kidney stones, arthritis, bone loss and osteoporosis are all associated with too much animal protein.

Calcium

Calcium is another hot topic for vegans. Or should I say, people who know vegans. While most of us were taught that dairy gives us calcium, it's really quite the opposite. *Dairy, butter and* **all** *animal protein is acidic.*

Because our bodies are amazing at adapting, they are really good at neutralizing this acidity. Our bodies literally pull minerals and calcium from our bones to accomplish this. I can't tell you how many clients I've had that were ATHLETES and calcium deficient because their doctor told them to eat more dairy. Unfortunately most of them also suffered from osteoporosis. After switching to a plant based diet and incorporating high calcium foods, like **specific** types of greens, those clients were doing much better.

Vitamin D

Vitamin D is not necessarily discussed frequently, but I can tell you from experience in the mainstream Medical world, vegans are known for having low Vitamin D. I, once, had a naturopathic doctor respond to my diet with, *"Your Vitamin D is probably in the toilet."* I couldn't believe he said that to his own patient! But according to the CDC, Dr. Gabriel Cousens, and Dr. Deborah Dykema anywhere from 50-80% of Americans aren't getting enough Vitamin D. So this is something we should **all** be paying attention to.

Mushrooms are the best plant food source for vitamin D. Portobella's have the highest Vitamin D. Going outside and getting natural sunlight (*without* synthetic chemicals like sunscreen!) is a good way to get Vitamin D. The darker skinned you are, the more sunlight you want to get. For lighter skinned person's it's recommended to go out in the sun for about 15-20 minutes, medium complexioned 20-30 minutes, and darker skinned from 30-40 minutes daily. This should be sunlight between the hours of 10am-3pm, wearing *no sun screen*, ensuring your face, back, legs and arms are getting direct sunlight. Supplementing is also an option.

Dr. Gabriel Cousens talks about the difference between adequate nutrition (Vitamin D levels) and optimal nutrition. Vitamin D is extremely important for immune health, brain and bone development and affects the function of over 300 DNA programs. According to his recommendations, a lot of us require a lot more than the daily recommended dose of 600-1000IU. For optimal nutrition many of us require somewhere around 10,000-20,000IU. He sells a liquid, plant derived (not synthetic) source of Vitamin D3 that I take daily. You can find this link on my site, *www.bemoreraw.com.*

The Importance of Digestion

Getting your nutrition from whole, natural, food sources is always the best option, but in some cases, people may want to supplement. How do you choose the right supplement? Let's address this using one example: DIGESTION.

I recommend that **EVERYONE** take a digestive enzyme but not just any enzyme. Most of my clients say they were taking enzymes but didn't notice a difference. Choosing a good digestive enzyme (and any supplement) is important. In most cases, **you get what you pay for.** Just like a lot of junk food that's super cheap, there's a *reason* for that. A lot of inexpensive supplements are chalked full of fillers, lubricants and additives.

When you buy a supplement that's bargain-priced you're paying for less of what you wanted and more of those undesirable fillers. A lot of those ingredients can be more harmful than helpful, especially if you're taking multiple supplements with these dangerous fillers. Some of these fillers are genetically modified.

I've tried many different digestive enzymes over the

years. *Health Alliance Digestion Enhancement Enzymes* by *Healthforce* are the best and most effective digestive enzyme supplement, in my opinion and experience. They are the only enzymes that I've seen that give you specific dosages dependent on what you're eating. For instance, you don't need the same amount of enzymes for an apple as you would for a slice of pizza. I really like this. They are very strong and can relieve gas almost immediately. I take them daily and have used them for years. They are available for purchase on my site.

You can never take too many enzymes. Enzymes literally just **digest food.** If you take them on an empty stomach they will simply digest what's there. If you wake up in the morning with gas, you can take enzymes to relieve that. Enzymes will help relieve minor stress on your other organs so your stomach isn't working as hard.

Enzymes can help with overall energy levels. Contrary to popular belief, the tryptophan in turkey is **not** what makes us sleepy during Thanksgiving. You'd have to eat an INSANE amount of tryptophan for it to have a "sleepy" effect on us. It's all that gal-darn food! It takes ENERGY to digest food. When we overload our stomachs with food, it can make us sleepy. This is true for any kind of food. If you over eat even the most healthy food, it can make you tired. Taking a good digestive enzyme can relieve some of this stress and therefore promote overall energy.

Genetically Modified Wha?

A lot of people have heard of GMOs but they're not quite sure what they are. GMO stands for **Genetically Modified Organisms.** It is the process of injecting one species' characteristic (by way of bacteria) into a different species. For instance taking the characteristic of the shiny sheen of fish scales and injecting into a tomato so it will be shinier (that's a real example, by the way). It is completely unnatural and a far cry from cross breeding plants that have been done by farmers for generations.

I see "non GMO" on a lot of labels that don't need it. There are only a few GMO crops that we have to worry about when buying produce. Corn, cotton, soy, alfalfa, papaya, sugar beets (not regular beets found on grocery shelves) and Canola. Lately I'm seeing the "non GMO" label on things like tea and peanut butter. Those big funky words you can't pronounce on those labels of your cereal, bread, and favorite snack foods, *those* are genetically modified ingredients.

Genetically modified ingredients should be avoided as much as possible. GMOs are another way that can cause the colon's wall to become permeable. They literally *poke holes* in the digestive tract. Corn, along with a few other GMO crops, is actually **patented as a pesticide**. Corn and soy actually *release their own insecticide* that kills bugs by exploding their stomachs. If these foods were eaten once or twice a year, it may not pose a huge problem. But these GMO laden products are in most of our food products on the shelves.

There are a few ways you can avoid GMO's. One is to buy organic. By definition organic food does not allow Genetically Modified Organisms. A second way is to look for the *Non-GMO Project Verified* logo which is becoming more prevalent in leading brands.

55

Avoiding GMOs is pretty easy when it comes to eating at home. The best rule of thumb for eating healthier and avoiding GMOs is if you can't pronounce it, don't eat it! Teach your kids to *read labels with you* at the grocery store. Ask them what each ingredient is. You don't have to know what every little thing means. You just have to know what you don't know. As they get older and you get wiser, you can begin to learn together the damaging effects of these chemicals in our food.

Avoiding Genetically Modified ingredients when eating out is a little more challenging. A lot of places still use vegetable oil or Canola as their cooking and frying oil. Well, I got news for ya: it ain't made from a bunch of veggies! Vegetable oil is made from soy oil, which is super processed and obviously Genetically Modified. Canola oil is a super synthetic, toxic oil that shouldn't be consumed. Hexane is used in the production of it.

56

LIST OF HIDDEN GMO INGREDIENTS:
Found mostly in processed foods.

Aspartame

(Also Called Amino-sweet, Nutrasweet,
Equal Spoonful, Canderel,
Benevia, E951 (U.K. & European Code))

Baking Powder

Canola Oil/Rapeseed Oil

Caramel Color

Cellulose

Citric Acid

Cobalamin (Vitamin B12)

Colorose

Condensed Milk

Confectioners Sugar

Corn Flour

Corn Masa

Corn Meal

Corn Oil

Corn Sugar

Corn Syrup

Cornstarch

Cottonseed Oil

Cyclodextrin

Cystein

Dextrin Dextrose

Diacetyl Diglyceride

Erythritol

Glucose

Glutamate

Glutamic Acid

Glycerides

Glycerin

Glycerol

Glycerol Monooleate

Glycine

Hemicellulose

High Fructose Corn Syrup
(HFCS)

Hydrogenated Starch

Hydrolyzed Vegetable Protein

Inositol

Inverse Syrup

Inversol

Invert Sugar

Isoflavones

Lactic Acid

Lecithin

Leucine

Lysine

Malitol

Malt

Malt Syrup

Malt Extract

Why Organic

Organic produce is so much more significant than we think. For me, it doesn't take any body of evidence or studies to convince me it's not a good idea to eat food that was sprayed with chemicals by a man in a full body protective suit (*this is true!*). But lucky for you, there are plenty of studies comparing organic food consumed and persons living near the farms that are sprayed.

There are multiple studies comparing organic food to conventional foods. According to a study done by Rutgers University in 2008, organic blueberries in New Jersey had significantly more fructose, glucose, malic acid, phenolics, anthocyanins, and antioxidant activity. Another study done by a John Paterson, a biochemist at Dumbfries Galloway Royal Infirmary, and scientists at the University of Strathclyde, compared organic soups to conventional soups. Eleven different brands of organic soups and 24 different brands of conventional soups were evaluated. The average level of salicylic acid in the organic soups was 117 nanograms per gram compared to 20 nanograms per gram in the conventional soups. Salicylic acid and its anti-inflammatory traits has been shown to help prevent the hardening of arteries and bowel cancer.

There is a plethora of data revealing the serious health risks for those that live near or work in the fields of conventional farms. Cancers, diabetes, Parkinsons, Alzheimer, and amyotrophic lateral sclerosis (ALS), birth defects, and reproductive disorders are all prevalent in elevated levels for those working in or near these toxic farms. Respiratory problems, particularly asthma and chronic obstructive pulmonary disease (COPD), cardiovascular disease such as atherosclerosis and coronary artery disease, chronic nephropathies, autoimmune diseases like systemic lupus erythematous and rheumatoid arthritis, chronic fatigue syndrome are also common.

But what about those of us that live in the city who are eating these foods? *"Pesticides are hazardous to human health,"* says the Toxins Action Center. According to a Harvard study, pesticide exposure is linked to a *70% increase in Parkinson's disease.* It proceeded a previous study done linking pesticide exposure to brain and nerve damage on animals. Scientists have also discovered that certain pesticides can mimic and compete with hormones that are responsible for body development and functioning. Most **herbicides are known cancer-causing chemicals.** Asthma has become one of the most chronic conditions in children. There are extremely high links between pesticide and herbicide exposure and asthma. According to one study, the strongest links were when children were exposed during infancy before the age of four months. *"Children exposed to herbicides before the age of one were ten times more likely to develop early persistent asthma ...."*

How much are we being exposed? And are there safe levels? There are a few studies measuring the level of exposure to these toxic chemicals. I don't personally believe there are any safe levels. There just isn't enough data to find out about the long term effects of these chemicals on our bodies and health. We are essentially guinea pigs and will find out in this generation or the next, for sure.

In 2006, a study was done measuring the levels of two pesticides in children's urine. After just a few days on an organic diet, the chemical levels in the children dropped tremendously. When they went back to consuming conventional foods, there was almost a 1000% increase in the levels of pesticides tested. This study was repeated with adults and the results were quite similar.

These adults (consisting of men and women) consumed a diet of a minimum 80% organic food for one week and then switched back and forth, just like the children in the previous study. During the week where they ate mostly organic, the pesticide exposure was reduced by 89%.

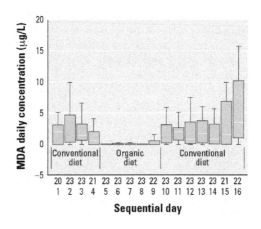

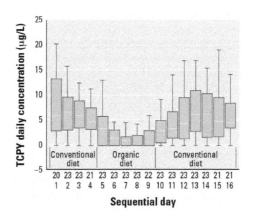

Environmental Effects

What does Agent Orange and our food supply have in common? Unfortunately more than you think. You might be wondering what the heck is this Dioxin she keeps talking about? Well, Dioxin is the **most toxic substance known to mankind**. Once it has entered the atmosphere, it does not dissipate. Agent Orange was comprised of two herbicides, one of which was a dioxin compound. It has been extensively studied since its appearance during the Vietnam war. It has been associated with not only cancer and diabetes but soft-tissue sarcoma, non-Hodgkin's lymphoma, Hodgkin's lymphoma and chronic lymphocytic leukemia, birth defects, inability to maintain pregnancy, decreased fertility, reduced sperm counts, endometriosis, diabetes, learning disabilities, immune system suppression, lung problems, skin disorders, lowered testosterone levels and much more. Dioxin bio- accumulates in the flesh of animals. It is found in highest amounts in fish, eggs, cheese, and meat. *The best way to avoid dioxin, is to eat a **primarily** plant based diet.*

Our US (and world) population is growing **exponentially**. It takes a lot of food and energy to produce that food to feed this growing number of people. The world population has been pretty much the same throughout history at a steady 770,000,000 people. Around the 1800s it began to increase and reached 2 billion by 1927. From the year 2000 to the year 2013 it has increased from just over 6 billion people to an astounding 7.25 billion. It took all of human history for humanity to reach a population of 1 billion but the next billion markers came in fractions of that time span, 2 billion in the next 130 years, 3 billion in less than 30 years, and 5 billion in 13 years.

Global warming is a real phenomenon not be scoffed at any more like it was a few years back. The problem with global warming and the greenhouse effect is the presence of too much carbon in the air. Annual emissions have increased from 6.5 billion tons in 1995 to an estimated almost 9 billion tons in 2007. It reached a new record high in 2013 of a whopping 36 billion tons. Forests actually do a very good job of *storing* carbon, however we are currently losing our forests at a rapid rate.

Saliesh Rao is a former electrical engineer, author of *"Carbon Dharma,"* and founder and executive director of Climate Healers, a non-profit organization that partners with school clubs and other organizations to educate the public. Their goal is to *reforest one-sixth of the green land on earth* which in turn will **negate the CO2 emissions**. He and his organization have been conducting research on the global climate change for over 8 years.

Mr. Rao allowed me to interview him and provided me with some astonishing numbers and conclusions. In the US there are 1.9 billion acres of land, 1 billion of which is used for livestock. Compare that to a mere 3 million acres that are used to grow nearly half of all the fruits and vegetables consumed in the US. Every year 50 million acres of forests are lost, 80% of which are due to livestock productions. Half of the forests that once existed on earth have been destroyed and half of **that** occurred in the last 50 years. These startling statistics are growing exponentially every year.

Because Saliesh grew up in India, where cows are considered sacred and therefore not killed, he got to view the damage this was causing first hand and at a faster rate than the other parts of the world. India is the number one producer of diary in the world. At one time it was comprised of ninety percent forests. Today **less than 7%** forest remains in the exotic country. India experiences this loss at a faster rate not only because they are the largest producer of dairy, but also because they let the cows live their entire lifespan of about 20 years. There exists about 320 millions of cattle which equates to about one for every four people. The US is on track to catch up to India's growing desert landscape.

As a result of watching his beautiful country's forests turn to ruins and making the connection between the environment and diary production, Saliesh turned vegan and experienced some pleasant side effects. All of his inflammation problems disappeared after a mere month of removing dairy from his diet (he was previously vegetarian). He suffered from joint pain his entire life and was on multiple medications for it. His arthritis and hemorrhoids faded away. He was soon **off all of his medications** because there was no need for them. He's not the only person I've met that had unintended health benefits from going vegan. Some people I've met had migraines disappear, acne clear up, more energy, softer hair and a variety of other subtle increases in health after going vegan.

Even just moving **towards** a plant based diet can have dramatic effects on your own health and the planet. If everyone ate just one less burger per week, it would be the equivalent of driving your car 320 miles less. If everyone ate no meat or dairy **one *day* a week** it would be as if we removed 7.6 million cars from the road. *Cowspiracy* is a wonderful documentary on Netflix that reveals startling statistics about the effects of the current food systems on the environment. It corroborates and supplements some of these very real numbers. It lists all sources on its site.

How To "Not" Go Vegan

The title, "Don't Go Vegan" represents not putting a label on yourself. Don't pressure yourself into something you're not ready to or want to do. I only want you to go vegan if YOU desire to and are **ready** to do it.

I'm so sick of meeting people that say they *"used to be vegan."* It's confusing and disappointing to me. It usually means one of two things. Either they did it as a diet or fad to lose weight because they heard it was a good idea. Or, they weren't successful and because they weren't eating the proper foods and ended up feeling sickly. But once you truly go vegan and make the connection between all living beings, your health *and* the environment, I don't think there's a desire to go back.

Look, I'm not here to tell you what to do. I'm here to tell you the truth and the consequences of our daily choices. If you want to go vegan, that's GREAT! But if you "fall off" and have a steak, don't beat yourself up. Just pay attention to how you felt after that meal. And if you feel guilty, ask yourself *"Why?"*. Ask yourself if you want to support the enslavement and brutal torture of other animals for your enjoyment.

So what constitutes going vegan and plant based correctly? Although the term "vegan" constitutes a lifestyle, it can also mean lots of fake meats and processed foods. I like the term "whole food, plant based." This diet is based on exactly what it sounds like, whole foods. This will get you towards optimal health.

Here are a few simple steps that can help you get healthy and or just lean towards a plant based diet:

1) ADDING IN

Add in a green salad with every meal, I mean EVERY meal. Even breakfast. I know a salad for breakfast sounds weird, but it can be a green smoothie. The point is, you're getting RAW, leafy greens in daily. This is where you'll get all your minerals, protein, calcium, iron, cancer fighting phytonutrients and plenty of detoxifying chlorophyll.

2) KNOW YOUR STUFF

Stay educated and know your stuff! READ, READ, READ YOUR LABELS! Don't be brand loyal. Companies get bought out and change. Always check your ingredients in your favorite products from time to time and ensure they are egg free, dairy free, GMO free and chemical free.

3) SWITCH IT UP

Eat the rainbow! Each color has different nutrients, vitamins, minerals and phytonutrients to offer. Eat as many different colors per week as you can. If you find yourself in a rut and eating the same foods, try to pick a new veggie or new veggie color every time you go grocery shopping. This can also inspire you to get creative in the kitchen.

4) SUB IT OUT

Take your current meals and look for meat substitutes. The options today have come a long way since the '70s. They are tasty, filling and some of them can fool even the biggest carnivores. All of your favorite foods are available in a vegan version. Lasagna, pizza, burgers and even eggs are ALL available in a plant based version! Of course whole foods are better, but this is still SO MUCH healthier than the alternative of consuming the flesh of tortured, toxic dead animals.

5) GET FRUITY!

Fresh fruit is great to include in your diet. It is full of fiber and water *(like all whole food, plant based foods)*. Fiber, as mentioned before, is important to help keep your intestines moving and regular. Fresh, ripe fruit is also very hydrating. Fruit is also a great way to ensure you're eating raw foods on a regular basis. Fruit as a snack or in smoothies is a great way to hide those bitter greens your kids may not like!

Your taste buds will actually change as you start to eat cleaner, more wholesome foods. You will actually start to crave those very foods. Additionally, as you eat better and begin to feel fantastic, if and when you "fall off the wagon," it will be much more noticeable how different you feel after that meal. You will most likely realize how much healthier you feel after eating closer to a whole foods, plant based diet, that you won't crave or even desire those foods after a while.

Field Roast Vegan Burger Follow Your Heart Cheese

Socializing Tips

Eating is so much more than food. Especially in America, food and eating surround *every* holiday. Easter, Christmas, Thanksgiving, Birthdays; these holidays are enjoyed by spending time with our loved ones and revolve around food! Well, what do you do if you're trying to make a change in a seemingly radical direction and your friends and family aren't?

Here are a few tips on how to handle those situations:

CONFIDENCE

Be confident in your answers and your decision. You're bound to get all the typical questions like, *"Where do you get your protein? How do you get calcium? Aren't eggs healthy?"* Know the answers and sources for these questions so you can dispel any misinformation and squash any thoughts about you being deficient.

LEAD BY EXAMPLE

Try to not be "pushy" with your views. I learned the hard way that if someone isn't ready to hear what you have to say, your words will be falling on deaf ears. Lead by example by bringing a healthy dish. A faux meat dish featuring a product like Field Roast is sure to please. Depending on the occasion, I don't like to share that the dish is plant based until it's eaten. I love to show people how enjoyable plant based foods can be and that you don't have to give up your favorite foods to be healthy.

FLEXIBILITY

Being flexible about your food choices doesn't have to mean comprising your health. Change takes time, but once you're in a place where you no longer want to eat animal products, by-products, GMOs and are focusing on organic ingredients, be flexible if invited out to eat. I'm not suggesting you abandon all your hard work, education and new ethics. But bending a little once in a while will probably not hurt you this one time. Enter each meal with gratitude and grace.

SUPPORT GROUPS

Having a support group of people who are like minded will relieve feelings of isolation when you're out with your friends and family. When I went raw vegan, joining Meetup and going to potlucks was CRUCIAL to my success. I was still bartending at a sports bar at the time being ridiculed for my daily smoothies and salads. I felt like I was completely alone and no one understood. Going to events and meeting like minded people reassured me that I was not alone. There are a *plethora* of people who live and think this way, too.

Can I Really Do It?

Today in 2017, going vegan is easier than ever. You don't have to give up ANY of your favorite foods. Burgers, pizza, lasagna, ice-cream are all available in vegan forms. There are plenty of options including brand names, recipes and tips for completely transitioning or just moving *towards* a plant based diet in this book. All of these brands I've personally tried and prefer over so-called "leading" brands. Yes, some of these are slightly processed, but they still come with OUT all the dioxin, cholesterol, and increased risks for diabetes, heart attack, stroke, hypertension and cancer. I invite you to try one today.

People ask me often, *"Don't you miss [insert favorite food here]?"* The truth is, I don't. I don't want Pizza Hut or Jack In The Box or Coca-cola anymore. I don't want those things anymore because I know the truth about what's in them, how they're made and what they do to my body and our environment. It's something I no longer want to consume or support.

During my 20s I ate and drank whatever I wanted. Ok, let's be honest; that was an understatement. I did a

LOT of drugs and drank just about every day for close to 10 years. I would go to Jack In The Box and Taco Bell and spend about $30 every time which is pretty hard to do with prices as cheap as theirs. Like most people in their early to mid 20s, I felt I was invincible. It seemed no matter what travesties I put my body through I came out okay in the end. But the fact of the matter is, these foods *are* doing damage to our body the entire time and it *will* catch up with us, sooner or later.

Change can be intimidating and overwhelming for most people. Take it from me. I've tried to show friends and family the information is out there to prevent, arrest or reverse heart disease and other chronic illness, but the idea of changing the food we love to eat is just so daunting. The fact of the matter is, even just moving *towards* a whole food, plant based diet can have astonishing health benefits. Having a professional Holistic Nutrition Specialist help you can be *extremely* beneficial for your long term success.

Ok, let's get things straight, I would love it if you went vegan. If done properly it can be a much healthier lifestyle and even if done *improperly*, it's much better for the planet and you're still decreasing your risk of cancer, diabetes, heart attack and hypertension. If and when you choose to live a vegan lifestyle, it's just that; a *lifestyle*. It is not a diet. It's about compassion towards ALL beings (not just our pets!). It's about not wearing animal skins or supporting animals in captivity. It's the belief that animals are not our belongings. And it's about saving the planet. It's a **holistic** look at how our food system, health, animals and environment are **all interrelated.** The point is, I want you to be *healthy* and *aware.*

Changing my diet and lifestyle has absolutely changed my life. I rarely get sick, my digestion is better, I'm more regular, I never get hemorrhoids and I have so much more energy. There's an entire community of vegans that I now know and can count on for support. I feel good about my food choices. I know when I make a purchase I'm supporting, promoting and encouraging a better world for not only all of us, but our children, and their children.

But, hey, don't take my word for it. Try it yourself.
Go plant based for 21 days and see how *you* feel.

Meet Will Tucker.

He's been training and competing as a professional body builder and athlete for YEARS. He has competed as a meat eater, vegetarian and as a vegan.

After going vegan his performance increased immensely and he finally began WINNING competitions.

Here are some of his **vegan** accolades:

2011 OCB Arizona Natural 1st Place Men's Open
2011 OCB Arizona Natural Men's Master 40+ 1st Place
2011 OCB Arizona Natural Men's Master Overall Champion
2013 Naturally Fit Supershow 1st Place Men's Master 40+
2013 Naturally Fit Supershow Men's Master Overall Champion

I had the pleasure of interviewing Will.

But there was really only **one significant question** I wanted answered.

I've come across multiple athletic and/or active persons that said they tried going vegan and they "needed meat" or they didn't feel good and it "wasn't for them." I've found myself at a loss when I come across these persons.

I asked Will, **"What advice do you have for these individuals?"**

Will: **"Your body will go through physiological changes when getting away from the standard American diet. Just hang in there and be sure that your nutrient needs are being met"**

Doing it RIGHT is essential and possible.
Just take a look at these guys:

THIS IS WHAT VEGANS LOOK LIKE.

TOOLS

Having the right kitchen tools will make food preparation exceptionally easier. Below are a list of essentials I have in my kitchen that I use *daily*.

- Kitchen Aid or Cuisinart Food Processor,
      with all attachments, 9 cup or larger
- Rubber or silicone spatulas
- A good, sharp knife (Henckels)
- Mandolin

The following are additional staples in any RAW kitchen.

- Excalibur Dehydrator
- Vitamix Blender
- Spiralizer

Wait on buying a dehydrator until you really see you're using it on a regular basis, simply because of cost. I use mine daily. However, I **highly recommend** the Vitamix blender. There is nothing on the market that compares to it. I wish I was getting paid to tell you this, but I'm not. It's just that good of a product. But you can buy them refurbished or used on Offer Up, Craig's List and Goodwill. They have 5-7 year warranties and are **well** worth the money.

There are also certain ingredients that may be new to you, but as you continue on a raw food or even whole foods journey, they will become common place and familiar.

These are staples in MY kitchen. Some of these are common in the raw food world, some of them are my personal favorites and shortcuts to making tasty, quick dressings or sauces.

- Coconut Aminos (Raw soy sauce alternative)
- Almond Butter or other RAW nut butter
- Majestic Raw Garlic Spread (any varietal)
- Coconut Meat - fresh or frozen
- Kala Namak (Indian Black Salt)
- *Chickpea* Miso (not soy based)
- Miyoko's Cheese (any varietal)
- Raw Coconut Wraps (on-line)
- Raw Cacao (not Cocoa)
- Coconut butter
- Kelp Noodles
- Kelp powder
- Agar agar
- Xylitol

What the heck is Xylitol? Sure don't sound natural to me!

Well, it is. It is a sweetener that is made from Birch trees.

Why is it so special? Because it has a **O** glycemic index. It is absorbed much slower and therefore doesn't turn into sugar that feeds disease, cavities or affect your blood sugar. It is COMPLETELY safe for diabetics and can actually help PREVENT cavities. Stevia is also great, but it has a bit of an after taste that can take some getting used to. Xylitol is a 1:1 ratio as a sugar replacement and has no after taste.

I like to keep a Xylitol simple syrup in my fridge as a staple. I use it as my "liquid sweetener" of choice instead of maple syrup or Agave. Maple is a decent sweetener, as it does have some health benefits, but Agave is super processed, NOT low glycemic (I don't know who started THAT lie) and has zero health benefits. If you must choose; whole fruits, Raw Honey, Maple, Stevia, and Xylitol are the best sweeteners, in that order.

You may also notice I use essential oils in a lot of recipes. They are much cheaper than fresh herbs that go bad quickly. The health benefits of essential oils is vast. If you decide to use them in the recipes, do NOT use store bought oils. They are not pure and it will even warn on the bottle, "Do Not Consume." After tons of research and experimenting with essential oils, doTERRA is the only company I trust.

Great essential oils you may want to keep stocked:

•Basil
•Thyme
•Oregano
•Rosemary
•Cilantro
•Black Pepper
•Cinnamon
•Cardamom
•Clove

I've chosen doTERRA for a few reasons:

PURITY - They perform 3rd party independent testing on the oils and even test the soil the plants are grown in.

EXCLUSIVITY - They offer products that I haven't seen anywhere else including beadlets which measure exactly one drop and even plant based supplements that have essential oils in them.

DEALS - They offer discounts and specials monthly on oils and other products.

FREE STUFF - Members can earn free oils and get all their shipping dollars back.

NO MINIMUMS - There are no monthly minimums **if** you choose to join and receive 25% off for LIFE.

You don't have to be a member to buy!
Oils are available for purchase here:
www.mydoterra.com/bemoreraw

If you'd like more information about becoming a member, contact me directly at
elizabeth@bemoreraw.com

CP**TG** Certified Pure Therapeutic Grade®
vs
Over The Counter Drugs

Peppermint	Lavender	DigestZen	Deep Blue
Pepto-Bismol	Neosporin	Pepto-Bismol	Tylenol
Tums	Tylenol	Immodium AD	Motrin
Energy Drinks	Aleve	Tums	Aleve
No-Doze	Motrin	Mylanta	Bengay
Tylenol Cold	Tylenol PM	Laxatives	ThermaCare
Sudafed	Sleeping Aids	Prilosec	
Zyrtec, Claritin			

Lemon	Melaleuca	Breathe	Oregano
Tylenol	Throat Lozenges	Inhalers	Nyquil, Dayquil
Motrin	Ear Drops	Vicks	Freeze Away
Throat Lozenges	Nyquil	Nyquil	Tylenol
Immodium AD	Dayquil	Dayquil	Motrin, Aleve
Pepto-Bismol	Neosporin	Shower Soothers	Throat Lozenges
Mylanta, Tums	Ricola	Vaporizer Refills	Pepto-Bismol
Children's Tylenol & Motrin			Tums, Mylanta

This is just the beginning...
Fill your home medicine cabinet with safe, pure and effective doTERRA CPTG Essential Oils.

SOAKING NUTS AND SEEDS

Nuts and seeds are extremely healthy forms of fat, protein, fiber, and plenty of minerals. But there's one problem. Digestion and assimilation of those vital nutrients is compromised.

All nuts and seeds contain enzyme inhibitors. These literally inhibit enzyme action. This means your body is literally fighting the food itself it's trying to digest.

Soaking nuts and seeds remove enzyme inhibitors, in addition to the phytic acid which is not ideal for digestion. This makes the amazing nutrients more bio-available and also MULTIPLIES their nutrition **eight up to fifty times.**

So how do you soak your nuts and seeds? Every nut and seed has a different soak time. But it's not as complicated as you think. The easiest way is to soak them over night.

Does this mean I have to eat soft, wet nuts (*get your mind out of the gutter!*). NO. When you're done soaking your nuts and seeds, you can dehydrate them overnight or use your oven with the door open at around 80-100° for few hours.

How To Soak

•Place nut/seeds in preferably *glass* container with lid.

•Fill with *filtered* water, just more than amount of nuts/ seeds. The nuts and seeds will expand.

•For almonds, turn jar on side or you won't be able to get them out as they expand.

•Next morning, rinse (with filtered water) until water is clear.

•Dehydrate nuts or seeds overnight or until dry (optional, depending on recipe/preference).

Some recipes will call for soaked nuts. If you have a high powered blender, like a Vitamix, (even though recommended) you do not need to soak if you are short on time. If you have a regular blender, soaking your nuts may be essential to making the recipe properly.

RECIPES

Xylitol Simple Syrup

1 C Xylitol
1 C water

1) Warm water and Xylitol until completely dissolved.
2) Chill and store in fridge.

You can multiply this recipe and make a large batch and store it for a long time. It won't go bad, but it will eventually crystallize, like sugar.

Single Serving Cream Of Rosemary Potato

(multiply recipe for larger portions)

CREAM
1/2 stick vegan butter (I used Melt Organic)
3/4 C almond milk, or similar
+1 C almond milk (divided)
1/2 white onion, chopped
3 garlic cloves
1/3 C nutritional yeast
1/2 TBS white pepper
1/8 tsp mustard powder
1/2 tsp smoked paprika
5 drops doTERRA Rosemary Essential Oil

'TATERS
1 C small diced or thinly sliced potatoes
1/4 C white onion, thinly sliced
2 TBS Refined Coconut Oil
Sea salt and pepper to taste

CREAM
1) Simmer all cream ingredients except Essential Oil for 15 minutes.
2) Remove from heat and let cool slightly.
3) After mixture is cool enough, add an additional cup of almond milk and Rosemary Essential Oil. Set aside.

'TATERS
1) Sauté until golden brown.
2) Add blended mixture to pan and put on low-medium until desired thickness has been achieved.
3) Garnish with fresh basil, tomato or Follow Your Heart Sour Cream!

Ground "Beef" Tacos

"Beef"
2 links Mexican Chipotle Field Roast Sausage
(or mix with Italian Field Roast Sausage for less spicy)

Fixin's
Daiya Farmhouse Block Cheddar Cheese - grated
Romaine lettuce - chopped/shredded
Diced tomatoes - diced
Follow Your Heart Sour Cream OR Cashew Sour Cream

Guacamole
3-5 RIPE avocados
1/4 C Minced Cilantro
Juice from 1 lime
Juice from 1 lemon
2 TBS Minced red onion
Salt to taste
Optional: kelp sprinkles

1) Start pan on medium-high heat.
2) Crumble in 2-3 links of Filed Roast Sausage of either Chipotle or half Chipotle and half Italian.
You may also just use Italian in which case add in 1-2 TBS Chili powder.
3) Sauté for 3-5 mins.
4) Turn off heat. Set aside.

Make Guacamole!
1) Mash avocados with fork in bowl.
2) Stir in remaining ingredients until well incorporated.

ASSEMBLE TACOS AND STUFF YO FACE!

These have fooled many meat eaters and I'm sure you can, too.
Don't tell 'em it's not beef until after they've eaten it!

Chili Cheese Fries with
the PERFECT tater wedges

1 bag or 1 1/2 lbs medium potatoes
refined coconut oil
1 TBS smoke paprika
1 TBS nutritional yeast
1-2 TBS garlic powder
salt and pepper to taste

1) Pre-heat oven to 425°.
2) Slice your potatoes into wedges by first slicing them in half, length-wise. Then slice into thirds.

3) Put all wedges in a bowl with melted refined coconut oil and spices. Toss until well covered.
4) Place on cookie sheet and bake for about 25 minutes. Test 2 or 3 of the largest ones to make sure they are cooked through. If they have nice, crispy, brown edges they are probably done.

CHEESE - Blend until smooth
    1 C cashews (soaked if no Vitamix)
    1 TBS lemon juice
    3/4 tsp smoked paprika
    1 tsp onion powder
    ½ tsp white pepper
    ½ tsp garlic powder
    ½ tsp salt
    ½ C red bell pepper
    ½ C nutritional yeast
    1/3 C water - add a little at a time depending on desired thickness

Philly Cheesesteak

2 thinly sliced Portobella mushrooms
1 thinly sliced red bell pepper
1/2 thinly sliced red or white onion
1 TBS refined coconut oil or vegan butter
1/2 C coconut aminos
3 TBS chili powder
1 tsp smoked paprika
1 TBS garlic powder
salt and pepper to taste

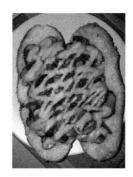

1) Put oil or butter in pan and start cooking down your shrooms.
They will cook down quite a bit, so we want to get these going just a little earlier than the rest of the veggies. Cook these down for about 5-7 minutes.

2) Add in remaining ingredients including all spices. This is where the magic happens.

3) Reduce this down until the coconut aminos has become to a nice, thick sauce. Keep an eye on it and add more aminos or water if the pan gets dry. But add very little liquid at a time, because we don't want a thin, watery mess.

4) When it looks finished (mushrooms and peppers are cooked down), turn off the heat, and if you desire, top with 2 slices of Follow Your Heart Provolone Cheese and put a lid on it. This will melt your cheese and make this ooey, gooey, savory, bold Philly complete.
Serve on your favorite organic hoagie bun.

To make cheese sauce, Melt 1 cup shredded Follow Your Heart cheese, 1/2 stick vegan butter and 1/2 cup milk in a sauce pan and stir, stir, stir. Stir forever until it melts. This sauce thickens quite a bit in the fridge to a weird consistency, so I do not recommend saving it for later.

Chili Dogs

This is a quick, easy chili that is packed full of flavor. It can be eaten alone, but it's great on dogs!

2 Field Roast Frankfurters
Daiya Medium Cheddar Style Farmhouse Block - shredded
(Don't get the regular, bagged Daiya shredded cheese!)
1 box or pouch kidney or black beans *(NEVER buy canned)*
1 white onion - chopped
1 red bell pepper
small handful of cilantro and/or green onion minced
2 TBS organic Ketchup
2 TBS organic BBQ Sauce
3 TBS Chili powder
1 TBS garlic powder
1/4 tsp salt
1/4 C water

1) Boil or sauté your dogs while you start the chili and they should be done at the same time.

2) Start your pan on medium heat and sauté your peppers on and onions until soft, about 10 or less minutes.

3) Throw in remaining ingredients INCLUDING liquid from the boxed or pouched beans. This liquid will help make our thick chili sauce.

4) Shred your cheese while letting chili cook down.

5) THAT'S IT! Let it reduce. Toast your buns, top your dog and add your cheese.

To make this a MEATY chili, crumble one link of Field Roast Italian Sausage into pan to start.

Vegan Wonton Wrappers

You can always use pre-made, but these are fairly easy to make.

1 cup flour
1/4 teaspoon salt
1/4 cup warm water
organic cornstarch or more flour for surface

1) Mix all ingredients except organic cornstarch.
2) Knead dough on surface powdered with cornstarch until smooth. Cover with a towel and let stand for 20 minutes.
Roll out as thin as you can. Cut with a ring-mold or cookie cutter into 3x3" circles.

Now the filling....

Vegan "Pork" Potstickers

These surprisingly taste like the real thing. I'm talking Chinese take-out potstickers. These may look involved, but they're DAMN GOOD.

4 garlic cloves
1/2 red onion, minced
1 Portobella mushroom cap
1/4 C cilantro, chopped + 1 TBS for garnish
1/4 C fresh basil, chopped
3 links Field Roast Breakfast Sausage, crumbled (trust me)
1 TBS fresh ginger, minced
1/8 tsp red chili flakes
1/8 tsp cumin
1/8 tsp chili powder
juice from 1 lime
2 TBS Coconut Aminos
3 TBS chiffonade kale
Salt to taste

1) Start pan on medium-high heat. Add REFINED coconut oil (or Avocado oil, which you can find a big bottle at Costco for about 9 bucks.)
2) Add garlic, onion and sauté for 3 mins or until soft.
3) Add in mushroom, "sausage", ginger, spices and sauté for another 2-3 minutes before finishing with fresh herbs. Mix in well.
4) Turn off heat. Add liquids, kale and mix well.
5) Fill small bowl with filtered water for sealing. Place a heaping TBS of filling into wonton wrappers and seal close with water. Press close with two fingers and thumb.
6) Put enough oil in pan to cover surface + a little more. Place sealed pot-stickers in pan and fry about 45 seconds. Then CAREFULLY put a teeny, tiny bit of water in pan then cover IMMEDIATELY. Oil and water do not mix, as you know. This method is used by chefs to steam.
Steam for about one minute, then remove and place on paper towels to absorb residual oil.

Traditionally these are fried so they're crispy on the bottom and them steamed to cook the rest of the way through. But if that sounds daunting, just frying them or just steaming them will still make for tasty pot-stickers!

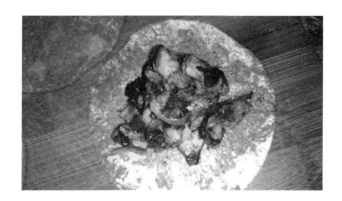

The Best Raw Burgers

2 C walnuts, soaked overnight
1/3 C sun dried tomatoes, soaked at least 3 hours (or overnight)
1/2 C minced celery
1/4 C fresh cilantro or basil
1 whole, ripe tomato
2 tsp coriander
1 tsp cumin
1/2 TBS garlic powder
1/3 C diced green onion
2 TBS chili powder

1) Pulse nuts in food processor until broken down. The level of chunkiness you want can be determined here.

2) Add in remaining ingredients process until well mixed. The texture should be a little moist, but not too wet. If it is too dry, add a little water or lemon juice, but just enough to facilitate blending.

3) Scoop out about 3 TBS at a time. Shape into a patty and dehydrate on teflexx for 3 hours at 125°.

4) Remove from teflexx and finish dehydrating on mesh screens for another 6-8 hours. We want these still slightly moist, but not wet on the inside. If you break off a piece and it still looks wet on the inside, let them go a little longer (another hour or so).

5) Serve in bread or over a bed of greens with tomato and red onion. These are awesome, warm out of the dehydrator and super filling. The creamy, raw mayo is also a great topping!

These will keep in the fridge for about a week, but I doubt they'll last that long!

Raw Vegan "Toona" Salad
with creamy mayo

1 C sunflower seeds, soaked for 2 hours
1/2 C pumpkin seeds, soaked and dehydrated
1 TBS lemon juice
1/2 C red onion, minced
1/2 C celery, chopped fine
1/2 tsp dried dill
1 tsp garlic powder
1/4 tsp white pepper
1/8 tsp mustard powder
pinch of salt

1) Place all ingredients except celery and onion in food processor and pulse until slightly chunky. You can process this more if you want more of a pate texture or less if you still want a little crunch. Either way, the flavor is great.

This recipe can stand on it's own if you want to keep it nut free, but when tossed with the creamy mayo, it really balances out the flavors nicely.

I like having this with some tomato and avocado over a bed of greens. It's also really great in a wrap! Super filling and simple to make.

Creamy mayo

1 1/2 C cashews, soaked
2 TBS ACV
1/4 tsp mustard powder
3 TBS olive oil
2 TBS lemon juice
2 TBS Xylitol Simple Syrup
3 or more TBS of water depending on level of thickness desired

1) Blend all ingredients in high powered blender until super smooth! Add the water a little at a time, just enough to facilitate blending. This, like all nut based sauces, will thicken in the fridge. So if you find it's too "runny," don't worry! Just chill it for a bit. It will be fine.

Raw Coconut Curry Soup

1 1/2 C coconut meat (or meat from 1 coconut)
1 thumb of fresh ginger
1 thumb of fresh turmeric
1/2 - 1 tsp red pepper flakes
1 TBS curry powder
1/2 tsp black pepper
1 tsp cumin
2 C drinking water

1) Blend all ingredients until smooth. You may blend for a longer period of time if you want this soup warm. You may also heat on stove at lowest setting. As long as it is not too warm to touch, then it is still raw.

You may add kelp noodles or zucchini noodles to make this more filling.

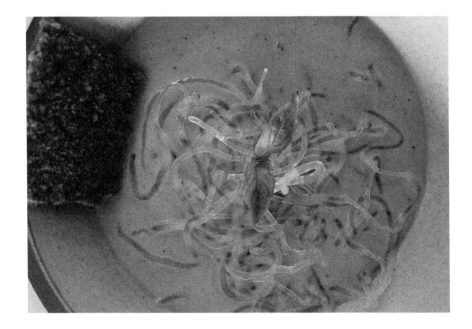

Raw Vegan Buffalo Cauliflower Bites

The variances in this recipe are so you can make this sauce as spicy or less spicy, as you can handle.

1 head of cauliflower, chopped into bite sized florets
1 C fresh tomatoes
1/4 Sun dried tomato, soaked in water overnight
1 TBS ACV (Apple Cider Vinegar)
2 cloves garlic (more or less depending on preference)
1/4 tsp cayenne
1 tsp smoked paprika
1-2 white onion
1 TBS fresh cilantro
1/2-1 TBS red pepper flakes

1) Blend all ingredients, except cauliflower, in a high powered blender until smooth.

2) Toss cauliflower florets in sauce until well covered.

3) Dehydrate overnight at 115° (or about 8-10 hours) or until desired texture has been reached. You may also bake these for an hour at 100° or lower.

Raw Pho

1 1/2 C water
1/4 C fresh cilantro, divided
2 TBS fresh basil, minced for garnish
1/4 C coconut aminos
1 tsp chickpea miso
1 TBS lime juice
1 tsp Majestic Raw Garlic Spread

1) Blend all ingredients until smooth.
Serve with fresh minced cilantro, basil and favorite veggies over kelp noodles.
This broth is good by itself, but the fresh herbs really bring this simple dish
home.

5 minute Raw Vegan Dressing
Adopted and revised from *Minimalist Baker*

1/4 C Majestic Raw Hummus or Majestic Basil Garlic Spread
2 TBS lemon juice
1 tsp garlic powder
2 TBS olive oil
pinch sea salt
Salt and pepper to taste
Optional: Nutritional Yeast and/or red pepper flakes

1) Place all ingredients in a bowl and stir!
Toss with your favorite salad greens or use as a spread in a wrap.

Raw Vegan Crabby Cakes

This recipe was an accidental recipe and sometimes those are the best.
I was so surprised by how much this simple recipe reminded me of crab cakes.
These are super awesome warm out of the dehydrator, but are still good chilled.

1/2 C walnuts,soaked
1/2 red/orange bell peppers, chopped
1 sm package (1/4 C) fresh basil, chopped
3 TBS water
pinch of salt

1) Process nuts in food processor until broken down fairly fine.
2) Add in remaining ingredients and process until chunky. If nuts are dry, you may need to add a little more water.
3) Dehydrate on Teflexx sheets for 2 hours at 135° (really just dehydrate them long enough so you can move them onto the mesh). Then remove and place on mesh at 125° overnight.
To really feel like crab cakes, you want these to be a little moist inside. If you over dehydrate them, they will still be tasty, but maybe not very "crabby."

You can enjoy these on their own and use the creamy mayo as a dip, cut up on a salad, or in a wrap.

Nearly Raw Deviled Eggs

Egg Whites
1 1/2 C pumpkin seed milk or similar
1/2 C water
2 tsp agar agar powder
1/4 tsp Kala Namak (Indian Black Salt)

Egg Yolk
1 C cashews
1/2 C water
1/4 tsp garlic powder
1/4 tsp onion powder
1/8 tsp mustard powder
1 TBS apple cider vinegar
1/2 smoked paprika
1/2 tsp curry powder
1/2 tsp dried dill
1/2 tsp Kala Namak
1/8 tsp white pepper

Egg Whites
1) Warm water, agar, and salt in pot on stove until it is COMPLETELY dissolved. Pour water into pitcher with milk and whisk a couple of times.
2) Pour this into molds QUICKLY about halfway. The agar agar will gel when cold. Place molds into freezer for a few minutes until they are set. DO NOT FREEZE! Keep remaining liquid warm. It it starts to gel, simply reheat.
3) Remove egg whites from mold carefully by pushing down from the top of the egg white. Do not try to push up from the bottom of the mold or they will break. Set aside until all molds are filled and egg whites are removed.

Egg Yolk
1) Blend all ingredients until completely smooth and creamy.
2) Place filling in piping bag if you want to be fancy or just spoon them out on top the egg white and you're done!
3) Sprinkle with paprika and/or dill for garnish and enjoy!

This is my number one selling item for catering and I can't tell you how many meat eaters I've fooled. NO ONE knows they're not real eggs!

Agar agar is a sea veggie that has gelatinous properties. It is FULL of health benefits.

Kala Namak, as you may have noticed when making this recipe, gives things an "eggy" taste and smell.

Best Pesto

1 C Pumpkin seeds
1/2 C cashews
1-2 TBS garlic (I like a lot of garlic, use your judgement here)
1/4 C fresh parsley, chopped
1 C fresh basil, chopped
1/4 C olive oil
3 TBS lemon juice
1 tsp salt
water - just enough to blend depending on desired texture

1) Place nuts and seeds in food processor and process until chunky.
2) Add in remaining ingredients and process until relatively smooth.
If you want a more pourable sauce, add more liquid. If you want a sauce you
can scoop out and use as a dip, use less.

THAT'S IT! Super easy and quick.

This delicious raw sauce can be poured over zucchini noodles or cooked pasta
for a "nearly raw" dish.

SWEETS

Awesome French Toast

3 Cups almond milk
3 Cups banana
3 TBS cinnamon
1 tsp vanilla extract (I prefer alcohol free)
1/8 tsp nutmeg
Your favorite, whole grain thick cut bread

1) Blend until smooth.
2) Heat your pan on medium-high.
3) Dip your favorite bread in batter (thicker bread works better)
4) Cook French toast until crispy with plenty of oil in the pan. Top with your favorite fruit, maple, or Xylitol simple syrup.

Raw Berry Purée

This can be used as a delectable dessert topping or a nice spread for breakfast.
This also doubles as wholesome baby food!

2 C frozen or fresh berries
1/2 dates

1) Blend all ingredients until smooth OR as chunky as you want.
For less sweet, omit dates.

To make this into a jam, add 1 TBS lemon juice.
Store in fridge for a week or so.

Raw Vegan Peanut Butter Cups

(These taste just like the real thing!)

CHOCOLATE COATING
1/3 C cacao
1/2 C liquid sweetener (must be room temp, not cold)
1/2 C coconut oil

FILLING
5 TBS peanut butter
2 TBS liquid sweetener
pinch of salt
2 1/2 tsp Nutritional Yeast

1) Blend all chocolate ingredients in blender until smooth.

2) Pour a little into chocolate molds and set in fridge to chill.

3) In the meantime, mix filling ingredients together in a bowl until well combined.

4) Remove set chocolate from fridge and add filling. Top with a little more of chocolate coating and chill until set. Remove from fridge and enjoy!

Raw Chocolate Ganache

This can be used as a topping for your raw cheesecake or an ice cream topping. That's IF you don't eat the whole thing up by itself!

1 C maple syrup or Xylitol Simple Syrup
1 C coconut oil (room temp, so it's liquid)
1 C raw cacao powder
1 C water
1 C cashews

1) Blend or whisk all ingredients until silky smooth.
Store in fridge or top your favorite dessert!

This ganache also pairs PERFECTLY with the Chai Cheesecake.
You could also pour this into molds or fill raw coconut wraps for brunch.
Just make sure it stays cold or it will melt!

Raw Chai Cheesecake

CRUST
1 1/2 C walnuts or almonds
1 C moist, PITTED dates
1 pinch sea salt
coconut shreds

FILLING
2 C cashews
1/2 C Xylitol simple syrup or maple syrup (DARKER the better)
1/2 C coconut oil
1/2 C coconut meat (optional)
3/4 C coconut water or water
1/4 C lemon juice
1 tsp vanilla extract
1 tsp cinnamon
1 tsp cardamom
1 tsp clove
1/2 tsp coriander
1/2 tsp ginger
1/2 tsp white pepper
pinch salt

1) Place crust ingredients into food processor and process until well broken
down. The mixture will start to stick together when stopped.
2) OPTIONAL: Place coconut shreds on bottom of spring form pan. This will
enable easier removal of crust later. Take date/nut mixture and press firmly into
bottom of spring form or any pie pan. Place in freezer to set.
3) While crust is setting, blend filling ingredients until smooth.
4) Remove crust from freezer and pour filling onto crust.
5) Place in fridge or freezer to set.

*This is really the base for ANY flavor cheesecake you want.
Remove spices, add in 1/4-1/2 C of fruit of your choice.*

SMOOTHIES!

This is the base for the perfect smoothie. It has been adapted from *No Meat Athlete*.

There are two options; the basic smoothie and the alpha smoothie. The Alpha smoothie is for those who need a hearty breakfast or are athletic and will definitely keep you fuller longer. It yields approximately two 16oz smoothies or one 32 oz.

BASIC SMOOTHIE

1 1/2 C liquid (water, coconut water, non-dairy milk)
1 soft fruit (banana, avocado)
1 C frozen fruit
1 C greens
1 drop doTERRA essential oil (lemon, lime, cinnamon, clove, Slim and Sassy Metabolic Blend)

ALPHA SMOOTHIE

Basic smoothie ingredients PLUS:

2 TBS fats and protein (nut butter, ground flax, whole nuts, oats)
1 TBS oil (coconut oil, hemp oil, Udo's Blend, Flax oil)
2-4 TBS protein powder

These are just guidelines and ideas
I encourage you to play around with your smoothie and find what works for you and
YOUR taste buds.
Ratios will always vary, as does whole, natural, fruits and veggies do.
So, don't be shy! Get blending!

Slim and Sassy
1 banana
1 apple
1 1/2 non-dairy milk
handful of spinach
1 drop Slim and Sassy
splash vanilla extract
optional: vanilla protein powder

Green Tropics
1 small avocado
1 mango or 1 C frozen pineapple
2 TBS coconut shreds
1/2 lime or 1 drop doTERRA lime essential oil
1 1/2 water or coconut water
handful of spinach

Peanut Butter Jelly
1 banana
1/2 C red grapes (or strawberries and grapes)
1 C milk
1/4 C spinach
4 TBS sunflower seeds butter

Cinnamon Pear
1 banana
1 pear
2 TBS oats
1/2 C spinach
1 C milk
1 tsp cinnamon
1 drop doTERRA Clove essential oil

Berry Green
1/2 avocado
1 C blueberries
1 TBS hemp seeds
1 - 1 1/2 C water
4 kale leaves
1-2 dates, if necessary

Island Breeze
1/4 C mango
1 banana
1 1/2 C milk
1/4 C coconut shreds or coconut butter
1/4 C pineapple
small handful of spinach

Purple Monster
1 C milk
1/2 C shredded red cabbage
1 banana
1/2 C pineapple

Totally Hot Pink
1 C shredded green cabbage
1 banana
1/2 C strawberries
1/2 C raspberries
2 dates
1 1/2 C water

Black and Green
1 C shredded green cabbage
1 banana
1/2 C blackberries
1/2 C blueberries
2 dates
2 C water

Be More Raw *Signature* Sweet Potato Pie

1/2 C sweet potato
1 banana
2 dates or 1/4 C Xylitol simple syrup
1 drop cinnamon doTERRA essential oil or 1 TBS cinnamon
1 drop clove doTERRA essential oil
1 drop ginger doTERRA essential oil
1/2 C almond milk or similar

This smoothie is amazing because you get tons of nutrition from the sweet potato and it's lower glycemic because it's completely raw! The **doTERRA** essential oils is this recipe make it anti-parasitic, antiseptic and anti-fungal.

You can also make this an apple pie smoothie by swapping the sweet potato for the apple!

To make this smoothie even creamier, add a 1/4 C of cashews (soaked, if no Vitamix).

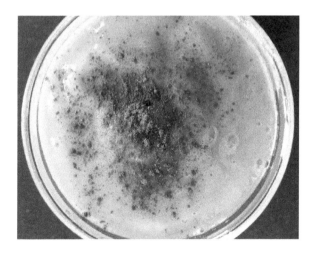

Chocolate Power

1 1/2 C almond milk
1 banana
2 TBS raw cacao or carob powder
1/2 C spinach
1 TBS cinnamon
2 TBS almond butter
2 TBS vanilla protein powder - HealthForce Nutritionals is AWESOME

If you want it sweeter, add a couple of dates.

This smoothie is awesome because it tastes like dessert for breakfast. You'll NEVER know there's greens in it! It's perfect for kids (as long as they don't see you make it!)

Be More Raw Signature Sweet and Spicy Adult Hot Chocolate

2 TBS raw cacao
1 TBS chia
1 TBS hemp seeds
1 TBS ground flax (or whole if you have a high powered blender)
1 drop each of clove, ginger, cinnamon, doTERRA essential oils
sprinkle of cayenne and black pepper
1 pinky of fresh turmeric root
1/4 C Xylitol simple syrup
Small handful of your favorite nuts/seeds - Pumpkin seeds, walnuts, cashew
1 TBS of your favorite green powder

Blend this until it's warm and frothy in your blender.

This is my morning breakfast drink after my green juice. I enjoy this DAILY.
It's perfect. It's full of fat, protein, omegas, micro-nutrients, macro-nutrients, anti-parasitic, anti-fungal, anti-inflammatory, good for circulation, cleansing, and it's chocolatey, warm and sensual!

If it's not sweet enough for you, add some more simple syrup.
If it's too hot, add more sweetener and cashews.

Appendix A

CHEESY.

There are other non-dairy dairy products out there, but not all of them taste that great.

These are products I've tried and have passed the "non-vegan" test at all my parties and events!

These are my personal pics.

COMING SOON

MEATY.

These products have been chosen because of taste, texture and INGREDIENTS.

There a lots of faux meat products out there. Most of which are heavily processed and/or don't taste that great.

These are my personal favs.

These make AWESOME pulled pork replacements.

RECOMMENDED WATCHING
Most of these are on Netflix and FMTV.
Some are on Youtube or their specific site.

Fed Up

Bottled

Vegucated

GMO OMG

Cowspiracy

Food Choices

Food Matters

Genetic Roulette

What The Health

Forks Over Knives

Human Experiment

The Beautiful Truth

An Inconvenient Truth

The Human Experiment

Fat, Sick and Nearly Dead

Super Charge Me! 30 Days Raw

Bethany's Story: The Power From Within

Simply Raw: Reversing Diabetes in 30 Days

RESOURCES

FMTV.com

lighter.world

happycow.com

rawmazing.com

bemoreraw.com

peta.org/recipes

nouveauraw.com

meatexcuses.com

phoenixvegan.com

onegreenplanet.org

fieldroast.com/recipes

followyourheart.com/recipes

gardein.com/category/recipes

Appendix E

References

"Reduction in Urinary Organophosphate Pesticide
Metabolites in Adults after a Week-long Organic Diet." Reduction
in Urinary Organophosphate Pesticide Metabolites in Adults after a
Week-long Organic Diet - ScienceDirect. N.p., 14 Jan. 2014. Web. 11
July 2017. <http://www.sciencedirect.com/science/article/pii/
S001393511400067X?via%3Dihub>.

McClees, Heather. "3 Reasons Egg Whites Aren't The
Healthiest Choice." One Green Planet. N.p., 1 Dec. 2014. Web.
<http://www.onegreenplanet.org/natural-health/reasons-egg-whites-
arent-the-healthiest-choice/>.

"Are There Side Effects of Egg Whites?." Are There Side
Effects of Egg Whites? | LIVESTRONG.COM. N.p., n.d. Web. 11
July 2017. <http://www.livestrong.com/article/156845-side-effects-of-
egg-whites/>.

Wanjek, C (2006-08-08). "Colon Cleansing: Money Down
the Toilet". LiveScience. Retrieved 2008-11-10.

Chen TS, Chen PS (1989). "Intestinal autointoxication: a
medical leitmotif". J. Clin. Gastroenterol. 11 (4): 434–41.doi:
10.1097/00004836-198908000-00017. PMID 2668399.

The 6th Annual Food Revolution Summit – (2017)

O'Keefe JH, Bell DS. Postprandial hyperglycemia/
hyperlipidemia (postprandial dysmetabolism) is a cardiovascular
risk factor. Am J Cardiol. 2007 Sep 1;100(5):899-904.

"Dioxins and Their Effects on Human Health." World Health
Organization. World Health Organization, Oct. 2016. Web. 11 July 2017.

"Dioxins & Furans: The Most Toxic Chemicals Known to
Science." Energy Justice Network. N.p., n.d. Web. 11 July 2017.

O'Keefe JH, Gheewala NM, O'Keefe JO. Dietary strategies
for improving post-prandial glucose, lipids, inflammation, and
cardiovascular health. J Am Coll Cardiol. 2008 Jan 22;51(3):249-55.

Csapo J, Peterfy M, Palfy E. Urinalysis in tubercular children kept on
Sauerbruch-Herrmannsdorfer-Gerson diet. Orv Hetil
1931-11-07;75:1090

Burton-Freeman B, Linares A, Hyson D, Kappagoda T
Strawberry modulates LDL oxidation and postprandial lipemia in
response to high-fat meal in overweight hyperlipidemic men and
women. J Am Coll Nutr. 2010 Feb;29(1):46-54.

Jenkins DJ, Kendall CW, Josse AR, Salvatore S, Brighenti F,
Augustin LS, Ellis PR, Vidgen E, Rao AV. Almonds decrease
postprandial glycemia, insulinemia, and oxidative damage in
healthy individuals. J Nutr. 2006 Dec;136(12):2987-92.

Cavalot F, Petrelli A, Traversa M, Bonomo K, Fiora E, Conti
M, Anfossi G, Costa G, Trovati M. Postprandial blood glucose is a
stronger predictor of cardiovascular events than fasting blood
glucose in type 2 diabetes mellitus, particularly in women: lessonsfrom
the San Luigi Gonzaga Diabetes Study. J Clin Endocrinol Metab. 2006
Mar;91(3):813-9.

Bornet FR, Costagliola D, Rizkalla SW, Blayo A, Fontvieille
AM, Haardt MJ, Letanoux M, Tchobroutsky G, Slama G.
Insulinemic and glycemic indexes of six starch-rich foods taken
alone and in a mixed meal by type 2 diabetics. Am J Clin Nutr. 1987
Mar;45(3):588-95.

Sun L, Ranawana DV, Leow MK, Henry CJ. Effect of
chicken, fat and vegetable on glycaemia and insulinaemia to a white
rice-based meal in healthy adults. Eur J Nutr. 2014 Dec;53(8):1719-26.

Collier GR, Greenberg GR, Wolever TM, Jenkins DJ. The
acute effect of fat on insulin secretion. J Clin Endocrinol Metab.
1988 Feb;66(2):323-6.

Wien M, Haddad E, Oda K, Sabaté J. A randomized 3×3
crossover study to evaluate the effect of Hass avocado intake on
post-ingestive satiety, glucose and insulin levels, and subsequent
energy intake in overweight adults. Nutr J. 2013 Nov 27;12:155.

Hätönen KA, Virtamo J, Eriksson JG, Sinkko HK, Sundvall
JE, Valsta LM. Protein and fat modify the glycaemic and
insulinaemic responses to a mashed potato-based meal. Br J Nutr.
2011 Jul;106(2):248-53.

Gerson M. Effects of combined dietary regime on patients with
malignant tumors. Exp Med Surg 1949-11;7:299-317

Appendix E

Arcaro, K. F. *et al* 1999. Antiestrogenicity of environmental polycyclic aromatic hydrocarbons in human breast cancer cells. *Toxicology*, 133: 115-127.

ATSDR (2000). Toxicological Profile for Polychlorinated Biphenyls. Agency for Toxic Substances and Disease Registry.

Carpenter, D. O. (1998). Polychlorinated Biphenyls and Human Health. *International Journal of Occupational Medicine and Environmental Health*, 11(4): 291-303.

EPA (2000). Hudson River PCBs Reassessment RI/FS Phase 3 Report: Feasibility Study. U. S. Environmental Protection Agency, and U. S. Army Corps of Engineers. Online at http://www.epa.gov/hudson/

Gray, L. E. *et al* 1995. Functional Developmental Toxicity of Low Doses of 2,3,7,8-Tetrachlorodibenzo-p-Dioxin and a Dioxin-Like PCB (169) in Long Evans Rats and Syrian Hamsters: Reproductive, Behavioral and Thermoregulatory Alterations. *Organohalogen Compounds*, 25: 33.

Jacobson, J. L. and Jacobson, S. W. (1996). Intellectual Impairment in Children Exposed to Polychlorinated Biphenyls in Utero. *New England Journal of Medicine*, 335(11): 783-789.

Johnson, B. L. et al (1999). Public Health Implications of Exposure to Polychlorinated Biphenyls (PCBs). Agency for Toxic Substances and Disease Registry. Online at http://www.atsdr.cdc.gov/DT/pcb007.html

Korrick, S. A. and Altshul, L. 1998. High Breast Milk Levels of Polychlorinated Biphenyls (PCBs) among Four Women Living Adjacent to a PCB-Contaminated Waste Site. *Environmental Health Perspectives*, 106(8): 513.

Mendola, P. *et al*, 1997. Consumption of PCB-contaminated Freshwater Fish and Shortened Menstrual Cycle Length. *American Journal of Epidemiology*, 145(11): 955.
Safe, S. H. (1994). Polychlorinated Biphenyls (PCBs): Environmental Impact, Biochemical and Toxic Responses, and Implications for Risk Assessment. *Critical Reviews in Toxicology*, 24:(2): 87-149.

Schell, L. M. *et al* 2000. Polychlorinated biphenyls and thyroid function in adolescents of the Mohawk Nation at Akwesasne. In *Proceedings of the Ninth International Conference*, Turin, Italy.

Stewart, P. *et al* 2000. Prenatal PCB exposure and neonatal behavioral assessment scale (NBAS) performance. *Neurotoxicology and Teratology*, 22: 21-29.

Weinand-Harer, A. *et al* 1997. Behavioral effects of maternal exposure to an ortho-chlorinated or a coplanar PCB congener in rats. *Environmental Toxicology and Pharmacology*, 3: 97-103.

Weisglas-Kuperus, N. *et al* 2000. Immunologic Effects of background Exposure to Polychlorinated Biphenyls and Dioxins in Dutch Preschool Children. *Environmental Health Perspectives*, 108(12): 1203.

Appendix F

Running Bibliography of Dr. Max Gerson's Work

Compiled by Gar & Christeene Hildenbrand of GRO and Michael Blake of the Francis A. Countway Library of Medicine at Harvard University, Boston, Massachusetts

Ahringsmann H. [Historische Bemerkung zu der neuen Diatehandlung der Tuberkulose nach Gerson-Suerbruch-Herrmansdorfer.] Munch Med Wochenschr 1929-09;76:1565.

Alexander H. Treatment of pulmonary tuberculosis with Salt-free diet. Munch Med Wochenschr 1930-06-06;77(23):971

Apitz G. Treatment of Tuberculosis of Lungs and of Other Organs with Salt-free Diet. Dtsch Med Wochenschr 1929-11-15;55:1918

Austin S, Baumgartner Dale E, DeKadt S. Long term follow-up of cancer patients using Contreras, Hoxsey and Gerson therapies. J Naturopath Med 1994;5(1):74-76

Axmann. Dietary Treatment in tuberculosis of the Skin. Munch Med Wochenschr 1930-09-25;77:707.

Bacmeister A, Rehfeldt P. [Phosphorlebertran und die Gerson-Hermannsdordersche Diat zur Heilung der Tuberkulose.] Dtsch Med Wochenschr 1930-03-21;56(12):480-481

Bacmeister A. [Interne Behandlung der Lungentuberkulose.] Med Welt 1930-04-05;4(14):474-476

Baer G, Hermannsdorfer A, Kausc. Salt Free Diet in Tuberculosis. Munch Med Wochenschr 1929-01;

Banyai AL. The Dietary Treatment of Tuberclosis. Am. Rev. Tuberc. 1931-05;23:546-575

Barat I. Gerson's diet in treatment of pulmonary tuberculosis. Orv Hetil 1930-08-30;74:877-879

Barat I. [Uber den Wert der Gersondiat in der Behandlung der Lungentuberkulose.] Beitr. z. Klin. d. Tuberk. 1931;76:588-591

Beck O. Herrmannsdorfer Dietary Treatment of Tuberculosis: Theoretical Basis. Monatsschr Kinderheilkd 1930-10;48:276

Bentivoglio GC. [Levariazione del riflesso oculocardiaco nei bambini in sequito al trattamento dietetico di Gerson.] Pediatria (Napoli) 1933-12;41:1457-1483

Bertaccini G. [Hermannsdorfer-Sauerbruch nella tuberculosi: richerche sulla influenza del cloruro di sodio nella infezione tubercolare sperimentale del coniglio.] Gior. ital. di. dermat. e. sif. 1932-12;73:1775-1778

Bertaccini G. [A proposito della dieta Gerson-Herrmannsdorfer-Sauerbruch nella tuberculosi; richerche sulla influenza del cloruro di sodio nella infezione tubercolare sperimentale del coniglio; infezione cutanea.] Gior. ital. di. dermat. e. sif. 1933-12;74:1469-1486

Blumenthal F. Treatment of Tuberculosis of Skin with Special Consideration of Dietary Therapy. Med. Klin., Berlin. 1930-09-26;26:1432.

Bogen E, Rachmel W. Pulmonary Tuberculosis– its dietary Treatment. Cal. & West. Med. 1932-11;37(5):292-296

Bommer S. Dietetic Treatment of Tuberculosis of Skin. Munch Med Wochenschr 1929-04-26;76:707

Bommer S, Bernhardt L. Dietary Treatment of Lupus Vulgaris. Dtsch Med Wochenschr 1929-08-02;55:1298.

Bommer S. [Neue Erfahrungen auf dem Gebeite der Hauttuberkulose mit besonderer Berucksichtigung der Gerson diat.] Strahlentherapie 1930;35:139-148.

Bommer S. [Beitrag zur Diatbehandlung von Lupus vulgaris.] Med Klin 1933;28:

Bommer S. Dietary treatment of skin tuberculosis. Am. Rev. Tuberc. 1933-02;27:209-215

Bommer S. Capillaroscopic study of skin following administration of Gerson-
Herrmannsdorfer-Sauerbruch diet in treatment of injuries to skin. Dermatol Wochenschr 1933-09-23;97(38):1367-1372

Bommer S. [Zur frage der Wirkung von Sauerbruch-Herrmannsdorfer-

Appendix F

Gerson Diat.] Dtsch Med Wochenschr 1934-05-18;60(20):735-739

Bommer S. [Salzarme Kost in Gefassystem (G.H.S.-Diat).] Klin Wochenschr 1934-10-27;43:148-158

Brezovsky. Sauerbruch-Gerson diet in treatment of tuberculosis of skin.

Budapesti orvosi ujsag. 1930-07-17;28:769-773.

Bruusgaard E, Hval E. Gerson-Sauerbruch-Herrmannsdorfer diet treatment in skin tuberculosis and its results. Norskk. mag. f. laegevidensk. 1931-11;92(11):1157-1175

Bruusgaard E. [Uber die Herrmannsdorfersche Diatbehandlung von Hauttuberkulose.] Acta Derm Venereol 1932-11;13:628-642

Bussalai. [Ladieta di Gerson-Herrmannsdorfer nel Lupus. (Nota preventi). Con presentazioni di ammalati, di preparti microscopi e di fotografie.] Gior. ital. di. dermat. e. sif. (supp.fasc.1) 1931;1:10-13

Canal Feijoo EJ. [Regimen acido como tratamiento de la tuberculosis pulmonar.] Rev. med. latino-am 1931-04;16:981-992

Canal Feijoo EJ. [Regimen acido como tratamiento de la tuberculosis pulmonar.] Rev. espan. de . med. y cir 1933-03;16:124-128

Cassileth BR. Sounding Boards: After Laetrile, What? N Engl J Med 1982-06-17;306(24):1482-1484

Cassileth BR. Contemporary unorthodox Treatments in Cancer Medicine. Ann Intern Med 1984-07;101(1):105-112

Cattell HW editor. Diet in Treatment of Tuberculosis. Internat. Clin. 1931;41(1):200

Clairmont P, Dimtza A. Dietary Treatment in Tuberculosis. Klin Wochenschr 1930-01;9:5.

Conrad AH. Lupus Vulgaris. Archiv. Dermat. Syph. 1931;24:688

Cope FW. Pathology of structured water and associated cations in cells (the tissue damage syndrome) and its medical treatment. Physiol Chem Phys 1977;9(6):547-553

Cope FW. A medical application of the Ling Association-Induction Hypothesis: the high potassium, low sodium diet of the Gerson cancer therapy. Physiol Chem Phys 1978;10(5):465-468

Cope FW. Mitochondrial disease in man: report of a probable case with successful therapy. Physiol Chem Phys 1981;13:275

Crosti A, Solari E. [Ladieta Sauerbruch-Herrmannsdorfer-Gerson nella tuberculosi cutanea; reperti clinice, biochimici, istopatologici (con dimostrazioni di fotografie).] Gior. ital. di. dermat. e. sif. (supp.fasc.1) 1931;1:13-16

Crosti A, Solari E. [Ladieta di Gerson-Herrmannsdorfer-Sauerbruch nella tuberculosi cutanea. Osservazioni cliniche e richerche biologiche.] Gior. ital. di. dermat. e. sif. 1931-08;72:897-945

Csapo J, Peterfy M, Palfy E. Urinalysis in tubercular children kept on Sauerbruch-Herrmannsdorfer-Gerson diet. Orv Hetil 1931-11-07;75:1090

Csapo J, Peterfy M, Palfy E. [Harnutersuchungen bei der Diat nach Sauerbruch-Herrmannsdorfer-Gerson.] Arch. f. Kinderfh. 1932;96:231-235

Curschmann W. [Einklarendes Wort zur ablehnenden Kritik der Ernahrungsbehandlung der Tuberkulose. Erwiderungen auf die Aufsatze von Sauerbruch und Herrmannsdorfer.] Munch Med Wochenschr 1930-12-19;77:2196.

Curschmann W. [Ergenbnisse salzloser Diatbehandlung nach Sauerbruch und Hermannsdorfer bei Lungentuberkulose und Knochentuberkulose.] Beitr. z. Klin. d. Tuberk. 1932;77:540-590

Curschmann W. [Beobachtungen bei Gersonsche Diat.] Beitr. a. Klin. d. Tuberk. 1932-01-17;80:120-131

Danholt N. Culture of Tubercle Bacilli from Lupus Lesions of Patients Under the Gerson Herrmannsdorfer-Sauerbruch Diet. Acta Derm Venereol 1932-11;13:617

Directives. [Richtlinien fur die Heilkostbehandlung der Tuberkulose nach Gerson-SauerbruchHerrman-nsdorfer.] Med Welt 1929-08-24;3:1229

Appendix F

Doerffel J. Clinical, Experimental and Chemical Studies on the Influence of Diet on Inflammatory changes in Healthy and Diseased Skin. Arch. f. Dermat .u. Syph. 1931-01-24;162:621

Doerffel J. Effect of a diet Low in Salt in Cases of Tuberculosis of the Skin. Arch. Dermat. Syph. 1932;26:762-764

Doerffel J, Goeckerman WH. Effect of a Diet Low in Salt in Cases of Tuberculosis of the Skin. Mayo Clin Proc 1932-02-10;7(6):73-78

Doerffel J, Passarge W. [Lokale Ektebinbehandlung der Hauttuberkulose bei gleichzeitigen Kochsalzarmer Diat (Gerson-Herrmannsdorfer-Sauerbruch).]

Dermatol Wochenschr 1934-09-08;99(36):1173-1179

Drosdek-Praktische. [Erfahrungen mit der Gerson-Sauerbruch-Herrmannsdorfer-Diat.] Beitr. z. Klin. d. Tuberk. 1931;78:697-723

Duncan GG. Diet in the management of ascites. Med Clin North Am 1932;16(1):243-249

Eckhardt H. [DieStellung der Kruppelfursorge zur Gerson-Herrmannsdorfer-Sauerbruch-Diat bei der Knochengelentuberkulose.] Ztschr. f. Kruppelfursorge 1935-05/06;28:79

Egues J. [Regimen dietetico en los tuberculosos pulmonares.] Rev Asoc Med Argent 1932-12;46:1574-1581

Elder HC. The Influence of the Gerson Regime on Pulmonary Tuberculosis. Trans. Med. Chir. Soc. Edinburgh 1932-11;

Eller JJ, Rein CR. The Value of an Equilibrated Salt Diet in the Treatment of Various Dermatoses: A Modification of the Herrmannsdorfer-Sauerbruch-Gerson Diets. N Y State J Med 1932-11-15;32(22):1296-1300

Emerson C. Treatment of Tuberculosis by Altering Metabolism Through Dietary Managment (Gerson-Sauerbruch Method). Nebr State Med J 1929-03;14(3):104-107

Evans WED. The chemistry of death. Springfield, IL; Charles C. Thomas; 1963:23-25,31.

Falta W. [Ist die Gerson-Diat bei Tuberkulose zu empfehlen?] Die Arztliche Praxis 1930;4:99-101

Falta W. [Richtlinien fur die Praxis. Ist die Gerson-Diat bei Tuberkulose zu empfehlen?] Wien Klin Wochenschr 1930;43(5):148-149

Falta W. [Ist die Gerson-diat bei Tuberkuloses zu empfehlen?] Aerztl.Prax. 1930-04-01;:99-101

Fishbein M ed.. The Gerson-Herrmannsdorfer Dietetic treatment of Tuberculosis. JAMA 1929-09-01;93(11):861-862

Fishbein M ed.. Dietetic Treatment of Tuberculosis. JAMA 1929-10-19;93(16):1237.

Fishbein M ed.. Gerson's Cancer Treatment. JAMA 1946-11-16;122(11): 645

Fishbein M ed.. Frauds and fabels. JAMA 1949-01-08;139:93-98

Formenti AM. [Studi sulla lipasi ematica nella dieta di Gerson-Herrmannsdorfer-Sauerbruch.] Riv Clin Pediatr 1938-04;36:319-350

Foster HD. Lifestyle changes and the "spontaneous" regression of cancer: An initial computer analysis. Int. J. Biosocial Research 1988;10(1):17-33

Francois P. [Leregime de Gerson-Sauerbruch-Herrmannsdorfer dans traitmtement de la tuberculose lupeuse.] Brux Med 1931-06-28;11:1034-1038

Frontali G. [Ladieta di Gerso nel trattamento della tuberculosi infantile.] Lotta Contro Tuberc 1934-08;5:818-830

Funk CF. [Einflusse der Sauerbruch-Herr-mannsdorfer-Gerson-Diat auf den Effektorenbereich der vegetativen Neuroregulation.] Med Klin 1931-07-31;27:1139-1141

Funk CF. [Zur Therapie der Hauttuberkulose unter besonderer Beruchsichtigung des Lupus vulagris.] Dermat. Ztschr. 1933-11;68:87-96

Gade HG. Preliminary communication on treatment with Gerson's diet. Med. Rev. Bergen. 1929-08;46:385-43

Appendix F

Gerson M. [Aus der innern Abteilung des Stadt. Krankenhauses im Friedrichshain zu Berlin. Eine Bromoformvergiftung.] Aerztiliche Sachverstandigen-Zeitung 1910-01-01;(1):7-8.

Gerson M. [Zur Aetiologie der myasthenischen Bulbarparalyse.] Berl. Klin. Wchnschr. 1916-12-18;53(51):1364.

Gerson M. [Uber Lahmungen bei Diphtherieban-zillentrazern.] Berl. Klin. Wchnschr. 1919-03-24;56(12):274-277

Gerson M. [Zur Aetiologie der multiplen Sklerose.] Deutsche. Atschr. f. Nervenh., Leipz. 1922;74:251-259

Gerson M. [Uber die konstitutionelle Frundlage von nervosen Krankheitserscheinugen und deren therapeutische Beeinflussung.] Fortschr. d. Med., Berl. 1922;42:9-11.

Gerson M. [Uber die konstitutionelle Grundlage von nervosen Krankheitsercheinungen und deren therapeutische Beeinflussung.] Fortschr. d. Med., Berl. 1924;42(1):9-11.

Gerson M. [Entstchung und Entwicklung des Tuberkulose Ernahrungenverfahrens.] Munch Med Wochenschr 1926-01-08;73(2): 51.

Gerson M. The origin and rationales of dietary treatment of tuberculosis [DieEntstehung und Begrundung der Diatbehandlung der Tuberkulose.] Med Welt 1929-09-14;3(37):1313-1317

Gerson M. [Korrespondenzen. Rachitis und Tuberkulosebehandlung.] Dtsch Med Wochenschr 1929-09-20;55(38):1603.

Gerson M. [Phosphorlebertran und die Gerson-Herrmannsdorfersche Diat zur Geilung der Tuberkulose.] Dtsch Med Wochenschr 1930-03-21;56(2):478-480

Gerson M. Comment on Wichmann's article of December 17. Klin Wochenschr 1930-04-12;9(15):693-694

Gerson M. [Grundsatzlich Anleitungen zur "Gerson-Diat".] Munch Med Wochenschr 1930-06-06;77(23):967-971

Gerson M. [Einige ergebnisse der Gerson-Diat bei Tuberkulose.] Med Welt 1930-06-07;4(23):815-820

Gerson M. [Erwiderung auf die Arbeit; Die Grunde der Abelhung der salzlosen Diat durch die Tuberkuloseheilanstalten von Prof. O. Ziegler.] Dtsch Med Wochenschr 1931-02-20;57(8):334-335

Gerson M. [Einiges uber die kochsalzarme Diat.] Hippokrates 1931-03;3:627-634

Gerson M. [Einige resultate der Diattherapie bei Kavernen nach vorausgegangener chirurgischer Behandlung.] Verhandl. d. deutsch. Gesellsch. f. inn. Med. Kong. 1932;44:222-224

Gerson M. [Blutsenkung bei Diatbehandlung der Lungentuberkulose.] Zeitschr. f. Tuberk. 1932;63(5):327-337

Gerson M. [Diatbehandlung bei Migrane und Lunentuberkulose.] Wien Klin Wochenschr 1932-06-10;45(24):744-748

Gerson M. [Erwiderung auf die Arbeit C. v. Noordens "Kritische Betrachtungen uber Gerson-Diat in besondere bei Tuberkulose".] Med. Klin.Wchnschr. 1932-09-09;45(31):1116-1117

Gerson M. [Psychische Reaktionen wahrend der Gerson-Diat bei Lungentuberkulose.] Psychotherapeut. Praxis 1934-12;1:206-213

Gerson M. Diet therapy of lung tuberculosis [Diatbehandlung der Tuberkulose.] Leipzig and Vienna; Franz Deuticke; 1934.

Gerson M. Liver Medications with the Dietary Therapy of Chronic Diseases. Wien Med Wochenschr 1935;40:1095

Gerson M. [Bemerkngen zum Aufsatz von Neumann "Ernahrung der Tuberkulosen".] Wien Klin Wochenschr 1935-03-01;48(9):272-275

Gerson M, von Weisl W. Fluid rich potassium diet as treatment for cardiorenal insufficiency. [Flussigkeitsreiche Kalidiat als Therapie bei cariorenaler Insuffizienz.] Wien Med Wochenschr 1935-04-11;82(15): 571-574

Gerson M. [Unspezifische Desensibilsierung durch Diat bei allergischen Hautkrankheiten.] Dermatol Wochenschr 1935-04-20;100(16):441-447

Gerson M. [Unspezifische Desensibilsierung durch Diat bei allergischen Hautkrankheiten.] Dermatol Wochenschr 1935-04-27;100(17):478-486

Appendix F

Gerson M. [Ruckbildung von Entzundungen bei Gerson-Diat unter besonderer Berucksichtigung der Tuberkulosen Entzundung.] Wien Klin Wochenschr 1935-06-21;48(25):847-853

Gerson M. [Anmerkung zur obigen Ausfuhrung von W. Newmann.] Wien Klin Wochenschr 1935-08-23;48(34):1069

Gerson M, von Weisl W. [Lebermedikamentur bei der Diattherapie chronischer Krankheiten.] Wien Med Wochenschr 1935-09-28;85(40): 1095-1098

Gerson M. Feeding the German Army. N Y State J Med 1941-07-15;41(14):1471-1476

Gerson M. Some aspects of the problem of fatigue. Med.Record. 1943;156(6):341

Gerson M. Dietary considerations in malignant neoplastic disease; preliminary report. Rev. Gasroenterol 1945-11/12;12:419-425

Gerson M. Effects of combined dietary regime on patients with malignant tumors. Exp Med Surg 1949-11;7:299-317

Gerson M. [Diattherapie boesartiger Erkankungen (Krebs).] Vienna; Scala, Hanbuch der Diatetik Separatabdruck; 1954.

Gerson M. No cancer in normal metabolism; Outcomes of a specific therapy. [Kein Krebs bei normalen Stoffwechsel; Ergebnisse einer speziellen Therapie.] Med Klin 1954-01-29;49(5):175-179

Gerson M. Cancer, a problem of metabolism. [Krebskrankheit, ein Problem das Stoffwechsels.] Med Klin 1954-06-25;49(26):1028-1032

Gerson M. On the medications of cancer management in the manner of Gerson. [Zur medikamentosen Behandlung Krebskranker nach Gerson.] Med Klin 1954-12-03;49(49):1977-1978

Gerson M. [Sind boden, Nahrung und Stoffwechselschadigungen grundlegend fur die Krebsentwicklung?] Ernahrungs UMSCHAU 1955;6:128-130

Gerson M. A New Therapeutical Approach to Cancer. Herald of Health 1957-04;

Gerson M, Hildenbrand GLG (Editor). A Cancer Therapy, Results of Fifty Cases. 4th and 5th editions. San Diego, CA; Gerson Institute; 1986, 1990.

Gerson M. The cure of advanced cancer by diet therapy: a summary of 30 years of clinical experimentation. Physiol Chem Phys 1978;10(5): 449-464

Gettkant B. [DieHeilkostbehanlung der Tuber-kulose nach Gerson.] Med Welt 1929-09-21;3(38):1320-1351

Gettkant B. [Lungentuberkulose und Gerson-Diat.] Dtsch Med Wochenschr 1929-10-25;55(43):1789-1790.

Gettkant B. [DieGerson-Diat im Lichten der Fachkritik.] Med Welt 1930-06-07;4(23):804-807

Gezelle Meerburg GF. Gerson-Herrmanns-dorfer diet. Geneeskd Gids 1930-04-25;8:381-392

Gibbens J. Gerson-herrmannsdorfer diet; summary of recent experiences. Brit. J. Tuberc. 1931-07;25:132-135

Gloor W. Dietetic Treatment of Tuberculosis. Schweiz Med Wochenschr 1930-05-17;

Golin A, Domenighini R. [Ladieta di Gerson-Herrmannsdorfer-Sauerbruch nei trattamento della tuberculosi infantile.] Riv Clin Pediatr 1935-03;33(3):257-300

Green S. A Critiqe of the Rationale for Cancer Treatment with Coffee Enemas and Diet. JAMA 1992-12-09;268(22):3224-3227

Grunewald W. [Unterscuhungen uber den Wasser und chlorbestand der Organe des tuberkulosekranken Menschen.] Beitr. z. Klin. d. Tuberk. 1933;82:189-206

Guy J, Elder HC, Watson CF, Fulton JS. Influence of Gerson regime on pulmonary tuberculosis. Trans. Med.-Chir. Soc. Edinburgh 1932-11-02;:1-5

Hagedorn K. [Vitamine und Tuberkulose. Eine kritische Besprechung der experimentellen und klinischen Ergebnisse, einschliesslich der

Appendix F

diaten nach

Gerson und Herrmannsdorfer.] Zentralbl. f. d. ges. Tuberk.-Forsch 1931-05-20;34(11-12):665

Hagedorn K. [Vitamine und Tuberkulose.] Zentralbl. f. d. ges. Tuberk.-Forsch 1931-06-27;34(13/14):809

Haldin-Davis H. The Dietetic Treatment of Lupus Vulgaris. Br Med J 1930-09-27;2:539

Harms, Grunewald. Treatment of Pulmonary Tuberculosis with Salt-Free diet. Dtsch Med Wochenschr 1930-02-14;56:261

Hashimoto M. [Uber die diatestische Behandlung der Knochentuberkulose nach Gerson, Sauerbruch und Herrmannsdorfer.] J. Orient. Med. 1930-11;13:54

Haught J, Hildenbrand GLG, (Editor). Censured for curing cancer: the American experience of Dr. Max Gerson. 2nd edition. San Diego, CA; Gerson Institute; 1991.

Henius D. [Diewirksamen Faktoren der Gerson-Herrmannsdorfer-diat und ein Rat zur versuchswiesen Anwedung.] Ztschr. f. Tuberk. 1930;55(4):319

Henry R, McLean S. A theory for cancer based on a study of cancer patients using the Gerson Cancer Therapy in conjunction with psychological counselling. Complementary Medical Res. 1989 Spring; 3(2):12-15

Herrmannsdorfer A. [Uiber Tuberkulosebehandlung durch diatetische Umstellung im Mineralbestande des Korpers.] Munch Med Wochenschr 1926-01-08;73(2):48-51

Herrmannsdorfer A. [Uber Wund – tuberkulosediat.] Jahresk. f. arztl. Fortbild. 1929-08;8(20):35-43.

Herrmannsdorfer A. Dietary Treatment in Tuberculous Diseases. Med Klin 1929-08-09;25:1235

Herrmannsdorfer A. [Uber Wunddiatetik.] Ztschr. f. artzl. Fortbild 1929-09-15;26(18):580-587

Herrmannsdorfer A. Dietetic Treatment Before and After Operation in Pulmonary Tuberculosis. Ztschr. f. Tuberk 1929-10;55:1.

Herrmannsdorfer A. [Lainfluencia de una alimantacion especial sobre la cicatrizacion de las heridas y sobre las afecciones tuberculosas graves.] Rev. med. german. iber. am 1929-11;2:677-684.

Herrmannsdorfer A. Differences Between Gerson and Herrmannsdorfer Diets. Ztschr. f. Tuberk. 1930-04;56:257

Herrmannsdorfer A. Effect of Sodium Chloride-Free diet on Tuberculous Process. Ztschr. f. Tuberk. 1930-12;59:97

Herrmannsdorfer A. [Zehnjahrige Erfahrungen mit der Ernahrungsbehandlung Lungentuberkuloser. Zugleich ein Kritischer Beitrag zum gegenwartigen Stande der Gerson-Diat.] Ztschr. f. artzl. Fortbild 1935-12-01;32(23):673-678

Herrmannsdorfer A. [Ruckschau auf die mit der Sauerbruch-Herrmannsdorfer-Gerson-diat erzielten Ergebnisse der Tuberkulosebehandlung.] Ztschr. f. Tuberk. 1952;100(6):316-322

Hildenbrand GLG. The American revolution in cellular biology. Healing Journal 1979;2(1):

Hildenbrand GLG. A new rationale for the antineoplastic effects of polarizing treatments. Healing Newsletter 1984-06;1:

Hildenbrand GLG. If it's so great, how come I don't know anything about it? Healing Newsletter 1984-09/10;3:

Hildenbrand GLG. Oxygen (part 2). Healing Newsletter 1984-11/12;4:

Hildenbrand GLG. Austrian's give natural cancer therapy a chance. Alt Med Today 1985;:

Hildenbrand GLG. Oxygen (part 1). Healing Newsletter 1985-01/02;5:

Hildenbrand GLG. Protein-calorie restriction in therapeutic nutrition. Healing Newsletter 1985-07/08;8:

Hildenbrand GLG. A case for reporting anecdotal cases. Healing Newsletter 1985-09/10;9:

Appendix F

Hildenbrand GLG. Has anything really changed? Healing Newsletter 1985-09/10;9:

Hildenbrand GLG. Imunity can be altered by (Pavlovian) conditioned response, hypnotism, and meditation. Healing Newsletter 1985-11/12;10:

Hildenbrand GLG. The trouble with alfalfa sprouts. Healing Newsletter 1986-01/02;11:

Hildenbrand GLG. Immunity can be improved by mediation. J Altern Med 1986-02;:

Hildenbrand GLG. A coffee enema? Now I've heard everything. Healing Newsletter 1986-05/06;13:

Hildenbrand GLG. Let's set the record straight (part 4). Healing Newsletter 1986-07/08;17:

Hildenbrand GLG. Let's set the record straight (part 3). Healing Newsletter 1986-09/10;16:

Hildenbrand GLG. Let's set the record straight (part 2). Healing Newsletter 1986-11/12;15:

Hildenbrand GLG. Let's set the record straight (part 1). Healing Newsletter 1987-01/02;14:

Hildenbrand GLG. Bread, propaganda, and circuses: Let's set the record straight, part 5. Healing Newsletter 1987-03/06;18-19:

Hildenbrand GLG. Comprehensive government report challenges NCI claims. Healing Newsletter 1987-07/10;20-21:

Hildenbrand GLG. Hoxsey film illustrates industry catch 22. Healing Newsletter 1988;24-25:

Hildenbrand GLG. A question of life and death. Healing Newsletter 1988;24-25:

Hildenbrand GLG. A best case review. Healing Newsletter 1989;5(2):

Hildenbrand GLG, Lindsay C. Eat only organic. Healing Newsletter

1989;5(1):

Hildenbrand GLG. FDA's Young says pesitcide problem not real. Healing Newsletter 1989;5(1):

Hildenbrand GLG. Nutritional superiority of organically grown foods. Healing Newsletter 1989;5(2):

Hildenbrand GLG. Pesticides: How big is the problem? Healing Newsletter 1989;5(1):

Hildenbrand GLG. When (at least) 20,679 Doctors were buttheads. Healing Newsletter 1989;5(3):

Hildenbrand GLG. Bomb threat quells cancer demonstration at OTA. Healing Newsletter 1990;5(4):

Hildenbrand GLG. Contemporary concerns in raw liver juice therapy. Healing Newsletter 1990;6(3-4):

Hildenbrand GLG. Cure of advanced (Duke's C) colorectal cancer through the Gerson cancer therapy. Healing Newsletter 1990;6(3-4):

Hildenbrand GLG. Freedom, fascism, and cancer. Healing Newsletter 1990;6(3-4):
Hildenbrand GLG. How the Gerson therapy heals. Healing Newsletter 1990;6(3-4):

Hildenbrand GLG. Cure of a recurrent, inoperable, chemoresistant mixed cell lymphoma (retroperitoneal lymphocytic/ histiocytic nodular diffused) through the Gerson Cancer Therapy. Healing Newsletter 1992;7(1-2):

Hildenbrand GLG. Cure of malignant follicular lymphoma (postsurgical recurrent, predominantly small cleaved cell type) through the Gerson diet therapy. Healing Newsletter 1992;7(3-4):

Hildenbrand GLG. Lupus, taming the wolf: remission and management of autoimmunity, systemic lupus erythematosus, in a young woman through diet therapy. Healing Journal 1992;8(1-2):

Hildenbrand GLG. Systemic lupus erythematosus: one disease, a thousand faces,

Appendix F

a potent management. Healing Journal 1992;8(1-2):

Hildenbrand GLG. Water. Healing Newsletter 1992;7(3-4):

Hildenbrand GLG. What has chemotherapy done for you lately? Healing Newsletter 1992;7(1-2):

Hildenbrand GLG. Will changing your mind help you heal? Healing Newsletter 1992;7(3-4):

Hildenbrand GLG, Lechner P. A reply to Saul Green's critique of the rationale for cancer treatement with coffee enemas and diet: cafestol drived from beverage coffee increases bile production in rats; and coffee enemas and diet ameliorate human cancer pain in stages I and II. Townsend Letter for Doctors 1994-05;

Hildenbrand GLG, Chair, contributing author, editorial review board. Diet and Nutrition in the Prevention and Treatment of Chronic Disease (chapter) Alternative Medicine:Expanding Medical Horizons. Washington, DC; NIH Publication No.94-066, US Government Printing Office; Dec, 1994.

Hildenbrand GLG, Hildenbrand C, Bradford K, Cavin SW. 5-year survival rates of melanoma patients treated by diet therapy after the manner of Gerson: a retrospective review. Altern Ther Health Med 1995-09;1(4):29-37

Hildenbrand GLG, Hildenbrand C, Bradford K, Rogers D, Straus C, Cavin S. The role of follow-up and retrospective data analysis in alternative cancer management: the Gerson experience. J Naturopath Med.. 1996;6(1):49-56

Hildenbrand GLG, Hildenbrand. Defining the role of diet therapy in complementary cancer management: prevention of recurrence vs. regression of disease. Proceedings of the First Annual Alternative Therapies Symposium:Creating Integrated Healthcare. San Diego, CA 1996-01-18/20;

Hildenbrand GLG, et al. The role of follow-up and retrospective data analysis in alternative cancer management: the Gerson experience. J Naturopath Med.. 1996-03;6(1):49-56

Hildenbrand GLG. Caveat Practitioner: the Gerson Institute. Townsend

Letter for Doctors & Patients 1996-05;:154

Hildenbrand GLG, Hildenbrand C, Bradford K, Rogers D, Gerson Straus C, Cavin S. Gerson diet therapy at CHIPSA: Discussion of evolution, rationales, and notes. Excerpt from Gerson Primer. San Diego; Gerson Research Organization; 1996

Hindhede M. Gerson's tuberculosis diet. Ugeskr Laeger 1929-11-14;91:1018-1022

Hoffschulte F. [Ergebnisse der Gerson-Diat bei Tuberculose.] Med Welt 1930-06-28;4:928

Holm E. [Versuche mit Gerson-diat.] Acta Ophthalmol (Copenh) 1932;10:232-236

Hval E. Microscopic study of capillaries of patients on Gerson-Herrmannsdorfer-Sauerbruch diet. Acta Derm Venereol 1932-11;13:593-600

Jaffe K. [Hamatologische Untersuchungen bei Hauttuberkulose warend der Behandlung mit Gerson-Herrmannsdorfer-Sauerbruch-Diat.] Munch Med Wochenschr 1931-04-24;78(17):703-705

Keining E, Hopf G. [Wirkt kochsalzzusatzfreie diat Tuberkulose-spezifisch?] Ztschr. f. Tuberk. 1931;62(5):352-356

Keining E, Hopf G. [DieBedeutung des Mineralsalzeinflusses fur die pathgenetische Beurteilung der Hauttuberkulose.] Dermatol Wochenschr 1934-10-27;99(43):1397-1406

Klare K. [Warum muss die Sauerbruch, Hermannsdorder, Gerson-diat bei Lungentuberkulose im allegemeinen versagen?] Dtsch Med Wochenschr 1931-05-29;57(22):928-930

Koehler B. Dietary Treatment of Tuberculosis. Munch Med Wochenschr 1930-10-24;77:1832

Korvin E. [Zur Wirkungsweise der S.H.G.-Diat, Kritik der Ausfuhrungen de Raadts.] Wien Klin Wochenschr 1932-01-29;45(5):144-146

Kremer W. [Erfahrungen mit der Gerson-Herr-mannsdorfer-Diat.] Med Welt 1930-03-15;4(11):354-356

Appendix F

Kremer W, Cobet G, Frischbier G. [Erfahrungen mit der Sauerbruch-Herrmannsdorfer-Gerson-Diat bei Lungentuberkulose.] Ztschr. f. Tuberk. 1932;66(3-4):185-203

Kretz J. [Uber die diatetische Behandlung der Lungentuberkulose nach Sauerbruch, Hermannsdorfer und Gerson.] Wien Klin Wochenschr 1929-07-25;42(30):993-995.

Kulcke E. [DieGerson-Herrmannsdorfer-Sauer-bruchsche Diat und ihre Beziehungen zur Lahmannschen Diat.] Med Klin 1930-02-07;26(6): 196-200

Lambotte. [Leregime de Gerson dans le traitement de la tuberculose.] Leige. med. 1930-01-05;23:1-2

Lana Martinez F. [Ladieta de Gerson Sauerbruch en el tratamiento de las tuberculosis cutaneas.] Clin Lab 1932-07;20:550-552

Lassen O. Gerson, Herrmannsdorfer diet in pulmonary tuberculosis. Ugeskr Laeger 1931-05-08;92:445-451

Lechner P. Dietary regime to be used in oncological postoperative care. Proc. Oesterreicher. Gesellsch. f. Chir. 1984-06-21/23;

Lechner P, Kronberger I. [Erfahrungen mit dem Einsatz der Diät-Therapie in der chirurgischen Onkologie.] Akt. Ernahr. Med. 1990-04;15(19990):72-28

Lechner P, Hildenbrand G. A reply to Saul Green's Critique of the Rationale for Cancer Treatment with Coffee Enemas and Diet: Cafestol Derived from Beverage Coffee Increases Bile Production in Rats. Townsend Letter for Doctors 1994-05;:528-530

Leersum EC van. [Phosphorlebertran und die Gerson-Herrmannsdorfer-Sauerbruchsche Diat zur Behandlung der Tuberkulose.] Ned Tijdschr Geneeskd 1930-06-07;74:2854-2864

Leersum EC van. [Phospholebertran und die Gerson-Herrmannsdorfer-Sauerbruchsche Diat zur Behandlung der Tuberkulose.] Munch Med Wochenschr 1930-06-06;77(23):975-976

Leersum EC van. [Phosphorlebertran und die Gerson-Herrmannsdorfer-Sauerbruchsche Diat zur Behandlung der

Tuberkulose.] Munch Med Wochenschr 1930-06-06;77:975-976

Leitner J. [Blutstatus und Blutsenkung bei der Diatbehandlung der Tuberkulose nach Gerson-Sauerbruch-Herrmannsdorfer.] Beitr. a. Klin. d. Tuberk. 1931;78:331-336

Levin OL. The Treatment of Psoriasis by Means of a Salt-Free Diet. Med. Journ. and Record 1931-08-19;134(4):179

Liesenfeld F. [Klinische Versuche und Beobachtungen mit den Diatbehandlung der Lungentuberkulose nach Sauerbruch-Herrmannsdorfer-Gerson wahrend 1 1/2 Jahren.] Beitr. z. Klin. d. Tuberk. 1929;72:252-259.

Ling GN. A Physical Theory of the Living State: the Association-Induction Hypothesis. New York, London; Blaisdell Publishing Company, A Division of Random House, Inc.; 1962

Ling GN. In Search of the Physical Basis of Life. New York and London; Plenum Press; 1984

Ling GN. A Revolution in the Physiology of the Living Cell. Malabar, Florida; Krieger Publishing Company; 1992

Lorenz GF. [DerKochsalzgehalt der Gersondiat. Entgegung aus dem Diatsanatorium von Dr. Gerson, Kassel-Wilhelmshobe.] Med Welt 1930-09-20;4(38):1362-1363

Lubich V. [Ladietoterapia della tuberculosi. (rivista sintetico-critica sulle diete gerson-Hermannsdorfer-Sauerbruch).] Lotta Contro Tuberc 1932-03;3:245-261

Ludy JB. Cutaneous Tuberculosis. Med Clin North Am 1934-07;18(1): 311-327

Maag. [Uber die diatbehandlung chirurgischer Tuberkulose nach Sauerbruch-Herrmannsdorfer-Gerson.] Deutsche. Ztschr. f. Chir. 1932;236:603-610

Maendl H, Tscherne K. [Beobachtungen bei der Diat nach Gerson-Sauerbruch-Herrmannsdorfer an 0 Fallen von Tuberkulose.] Tuberkulose 1930-06-10;10:132-134

Mariette E. The Dietetic Treatment of Tuberculosis. Ann Intern Med 1932;5:793-802

Appendix F

Martensson A. Gerson-Sauerbruch-Herrmanns-dorfer diet in treatment of tuberculosis. Ugeskr Laeger 1929-11-28;91:1063-1066.

Mathiesen H. Gerson's tuberculosis diet. Ugeskr Laeger 1929-11-28;91:1066.

Matz PB. Gerson-Sauerbruch dietetic Regimen. Med Bull Vet Adm 1930-01;6:27-32

Mayer E, Kugelmass IN. Basic 'vitamin' Feeding in Tuberculosis. JAMA 1929-12-14;93(24):1856-1862.

Mayer E. Salt-restricted Dietary With Particular Application to Tuberculosis Therapy. JAMA 1931-12-26;97(26):1935-1939

McCarty M. Aldosterone and the Gerson diet — a speculation. Med Hypotheses 1981;7:591-597

McKenzie V. Tuberculosis cure by diet is explained to M'Kenzie. The Times 1929-09;

Mecklenburg M. Sauerbruch-Herrmannsdorfer Diet in Chronic Pulmonary Tuberculosis. Ztschr. f. Tuberk., Leipzig 1930-06;57:47

Metz GA. [Uber die therapeutische Wirkung von Lebertrans, Sauerbruch-Hermannsdorfer-Gerson-Diat und Heliotherapie bei Tuberkulose.] Dtsch Med Wochenschr 1935-06;61(23):916-917

Meyer F. [Zur Gerson-Therapie (Medizinische Aussprache).] Med Welt 1930-01-11;4(2):68

Meyer M, Irrmann E. [Considerations sur le traitement dietetique de la tuberculose d'apres Sauerbruch-Herrmannsdorfer-Gerson.] Strasb Med 1932-03-15;92:169-171

Meyer M, Irrmann E. [LeRegime de Sauerbruch-Hermannsdorger-Gerson ses Base Theoriques ses Resultats Dans la Tuberculose Externe.] Gazette des hopitaux. 1932-06-25;105(51):957-961

Meyer M, Irrmann E. [LeRegime de Sauerbruch-Hermannsdorger-Gerson ses BaseTheoriques ses Resultats Dans la Tuberculose Externe.] Gazette des hopitaux. 1932-06-25;105(52):997

Michelson HE. Lupus Vulgaris. Arch. Dermat. Syph. 1931;24:1122

Mienicki M. An Attempt to Increase the Curative Effect of a Salt-free Diet on Lupus Vulgaris. Przegl Dermatol 1934-09;29:346

Moeller A. The Dangers of Salt Withdrawal in Pulmonary Tuberculosis. Dtsch Med Wochenschr 1930-08-15;

Monzon J. [Leregime de Gerson; un essai allemand de traitmtement dietetique de la tuberculose pulmonaire.] Presse Med 1929-09-25;37:1251-1254

Moreschi C. The connection between nutrition and tumor promotion. [?] Zeitschr f Immunitätsforsch. 1909;2:651

Moss R. The Cancer Industry: The Classic Expose on the Cancer Establishment Equinox Press; 1996

Muller P. [Uber die Behandlung der Lungentuberkulose mit salzfreier Kost und Mineralogen.] Dtsch Arch Klin Med 1927;158:34-41

Munchbach W. [Gerso-Herrmannsdorfer-Sauerbruch-Diat.] Beitr. z. Klin. d. Tuberk. 1931;77:395-411

Neumann W von. [Bemerkungen zu der Arbeit von Max Gerson in Nr. 25, 1935, dieser Wochenschrift.] Wien Klin Wochenschr 1935-08-23;48(34):1069

NIH Publication. Diet and Nutrition in the Prevention and Treatment of Chronic Disease: Gerson Therapy. Alternative Medicine: Expanding Medical Horizons 1994-12;94-066:

Noorden C von. [Kritische Betrachtungen uber GersonDiat, in besondere bei Tuberkulose.] Med Klin 1932-05-27;28(22):743-748

Noorden C von. [Bemerkungen zur Gerson-Diat.] Wien Klin Wochenschr 1932-06-03;45:708-709

Noorden C von. Reply to Gerson. Med Klin 1932-07-29;28(3):1062-1063

Office of Technology Assessment. Unconventional Cancer Treatments. U.S. Government Printing Office; OTA-H-405:1990.

Appendix F

Office of Technology Assessment. Unconventional Cancer Treatments –
Advisory Panel Meeting transcript. [source unkown] 1990-03-09.

Ota M. [Erfahrungen mit der Diatbehandlung nach Gerson-Sauerbruch-
Herrmannsdorfer bei Hauttuberkulose.] Jap. J. Dermat. & Urol.
1936-05-20;39:82-85

Oulmann L. Lupus Vulagris. Arch. Dermat. Syph. 1931;34:317

Pachioli R, Gianni G. [Contributo ala cura della tuberculosi polmonare
del bambino medianto il trattamento dietetico di Gerson,
Herrmannsdorfer, Sauerbruch.] Riv. d. pat. e. clin. d. tuberc.
1931-06-30;5:446-469

Pachioli R, Gianni G. [Richereche sull meccanismo d'azioine del regime
di Gerson-Herrmannsdorfer-Sauerbruch nel trattamento della affezioni
tubercolari.] Riv Clin Pediatr 1932-05;30:664-680

Parreidt R. [Behandlung der Paradentose durch Diat (nach Gerson).]
Osterr Z Stomatol 1929-10;27:969-972

Pawlowski E. [Erforhung mit der Gerson-Herrmannsdorfer-diat in der
Behandlung der Knochen- und Gelenktuberkulose.] Dtsch Med
Wochenschr 1930-10-31;56(44):1870-1871

Pennetti G. [Ladieta de Gerson-herrmansdorfer-Sauerbruch nella
affezioni tubercolari.] Riforma Med 1930-03-10;46:372-376

Pfeffer G, Stern E. [Uber die wirkung der Sauerbruch-Gersonschen diat
bei Lungentuberkulose.] Beitr. z. Klin. d. Tuberk. 1927;67:742-747.

Pinner M. Book Review of "Diatbehandlung der Lungentuberkulose".
Am. Rev. Tuberc. 1935;32:116-117

Pohlmann C. Influence of Gerson's dietary treatment Continued for
Four Months in Severe Pulmonary and Laryngeal Tuberculosis. Munch
Med Wochenschr 1930-04-25;77(17):707-708

Popper M. [Dermatoskopische Befunde bei Lichtreaktionen der Haut
unter dem Einfluss Sauerbruch-Herrmannsdorfer-Gersonshen (S.H.G.)
Diat.] Strahlentherapie 1932;45:235-246

Raadt OLE de. Gerson diet; factor responsible for curative value. Wien

Klin Wochenschr 1930-06-12;43:752-753

Raadt OLE de. Reply to Korvin's article. Wien Klin Wochenschr 1932-01-29;45(5):146-147

Reed A, James N, Sikora K. Round the World: Mexico: Juices, coffee enemas, and cancer. Lancet 1990-09-15;336(8716):677-678

Regelson W. The 'Grand Conspiracy' Against the Cancer Cure. JAMA 1980-01-25;243(4):337-339

Richards BA. The enzyme knife — a renewed direction for cancer therapy? discussion paper. Proc R Soc Med 1988;81:284-285

Rieckenberg H. [Gerson-Diat bei Lungentuberkulose.] Dtsch Med Wochenschr 1930-05-02;56(18):746-747

Ritschel HU. [Diediat nach Gerson in der Behandlung der chronischen Lungentuberkulose.] Deitr. z. klin. d. tuberk. 1928;68:394-398

Rosen K. Herrmannsdorfer-Gerson diet in pulmonary tuberculosis. Svenska. lak. tidning 1931-02-27;28:305-316

Rous P. The influence of diet on transplanted and spontaneous mouse tumors. J Exp Med 1914;20:433

Sachs W. [Diesalzarme Kost nach Gerson-Sauerbruch-Herrmannsdorfer in der Behandlung der Lungentuberkulose.] Beitr. z. Klin. d. Tuberk. 1930;73:816-824

Santori G. [L'alimentazione di Gerson, Sauerbruch e Herrmannsdorfer nella cura del lupus volgare.] Bull.e. atti. D. R. Acad .med. di Roma 1930-01;56:25-29

Sauerbruch F. [Allgemeine klinische Grundlagen fur Ernahrungsbehandlung entzundlieher Erkrankungen.] Munch Med Wochenschr 1926-01-08;73(2):47-48.

Sauerbruch F, Herrmannsdorfer A. [Ergebnisse und Wert einer diatetischen Behandlung der Tuberkulose.] Munch Med Wochenschr 1928-01-06;75:35-38.

Sauerbruch F. [Erklarung zur Ernahrungsbehandlung der Tuberkulse.]

Appendix F

Beitr. z. Klin. chir. 1929;147:501-502.

Sauerbruch F. [Stellungnahme zu Gerson unt Gettkant.] Med Welt 1929-09-21;3:1351

Sauerbruch F. [Erklarung zur Ernahrungsbehandlung der Tuberkulse.] Beitr. z. Klin. chir. 1929;219:381-382.

Sauerbruch F. [Erklarung zur Ernahrungsbehandlung der tuberkulose.] Med Klin 1929-08-09;25:1272

Sauerbruch F. [Erklarung zur Ernahrungsbehandlung der tuberkulose.] Dtsch Med Wochenschr 1929-08-16;55:1391-1392

Sauerbruch F. [Erklarung zur Ernahrungsbehandlung der tuberkulose.] Munch Med Wochenschr 1929-08-16;76:1363.

Sauerbruch F. [Erklarung zur Ernahrungsbehandlung der tuberkulose.] Zentralbl. f. inn. Med 1929-08-31;50:802.

Sauerbruch F. [Erklarung zur Ernahrungsbehandlung der tuberkulose.] Chirug. 1929-09-01;1:933.

Sauerbruch F. [Erklarung zur Ernahrungsbehandlung der Tuberkulose.] Zentralbl Chir 1929-09-14;56(37):2306-2307

Sauerbruch F. [Erklarung zur Ernahrungsbehandlung der tuberkulose.] Med Welt 1929-09-21;3:1351

Sauerbruch F. [Einklarendes Wort zur ablehnenden Kritik der Ernahrungsbehandlung der Tuberkulose.] Munch Med Wochenschr 1930-10-24;77(43):1829-1832

Sauerbruch F, Herrmannsdorfer A, Gerson M. [Ueber Versuche, Schwere Formen von Lungentuberkulose Durch Diaetetische Behandlung zu Beeinflussen.] Munch Med Wochenschr 1930;23:

Sauerbruch F. Master Surgeon (a.k.a. A Surgeon's Life) [Das War Mein Leben.] London, Andre Deutsch, 1953 [Muenchen ,Kindler, 1951]

Schade H, Bechk A, Reimers C. Physiocochemical Study of Action of Acid Food in Wound Healing: Effect of Gerson Diet on Wound Healing. Zentralbl. f. Chir. Leipzig. 1930;57:1077

Schedtler O. [Wirkt kochsalzzufreie diat Tuberkulose-spezifisch? Bemerkungen zu der Arbeit von Keining und Hopf.] Ztschr. f. Tuberk. 1932;63(5):337-338

Scheurlen F, Orlowitsch-Wolk A. Vitamin Therapy of Pulmonary Tuberculosis. Munch Med Wochenschr 1930-06-06;77(23):976

Schiff E. Dietetic Treatment of Neurodermatitis in Childhood. Archives of Pediatrics 1935-01;52(1):L2944-52

Schiller W. [Zur Frage der Kochsalzarme Kosnach Sauerbruch-Herrmannsdorfer-Gerson bei Tuberkulose.] Tuberkulose 1929-04;9:70-74.

Schlammadinger J. Gerson-Herrmannsdorfer-Sauerbruch diet in treatment of tuberculosis and chronic diseases fo the skin. Orv Hetil 1930-09-20;74:954-957

Schlammadinger J, Szep E. Gerson-Herrmanns-dorfer-Sauerbruch diet in treatment of tuberculosis and chronic diseases of the skin. Med Klin 1931-04-02;27(14):508-510

Schlesinger W. [DieGerson-Herrmannsdorfer-Sauerbruchsche Tuberkulosediat.] Wien Med Wochenschr 1930-04-26;80:587-589

Schmiedeberg H. Herrmannsdorfer diet in Tuberculosis in children. Monatsschr Kinderheilkd 1930-10;8:230

Schmitz H. [Uber die Gersonche Diat bei Lungentuberkulose.] Ztschr. f. Tuberk 1927;47:461.

Schrick FG van. [Haut und Knochentuberkulose unter dem Einfluss der Sauerbruch-Herrmannsdorfer-Gerson-Diat.] Ztschr. f. Orthop. Chir. 1934;61:388-394

Schroeder MG. Modern Dietetic Problems in Teatment of the Tuberculous. Journal of State Med. 1931-08;39:435

Schwalm E. [Erfahrungen mit der Gerson-Diat bei Lungentuberkulose.] Klin Wochenschr 1929-10-15;8(42):1941-1943

Scolari E. [Osservazioni cliniche e ricerche sperimentali sulla dieta di Sauerbruch-Herrmannsdorfer-Gerson nella affezioni cutanea.] Gior.

Appendix F

ital. di. dermat. e. sif. 1935-06;76:665-701

Sellei J. Gerson diet in treatment of skin diseases. Gyogyaszat.
1930-06-08;70:453-454

Silverstone H, Tannenbaum A. Influence of thyroid hormone on the
formation of induced skin tumors in mice. Cancer Res
1949-11;9:684-688

Sliosberg A. [Letraitement de la tuberculose par la methode de Gerson.]
Rev. de. phtisiol. med. soc 1929-11/12;10:564-574.

Sossi O. [Sulla cura dietetica di Sauerbruch-Herr-mannsdorfer nella
tuberculosi pu monare.] Riv. de. clin. med 1929-10-31;30:1124-1149.

Sprigge S, Morland E eds.. The Gerson Diet for Tuberculosis. Lancet
1929-06-28;218(1):1415.

Sprigge S, Morland E eds.. Dietary Treatment of Tuberculosis. Lancet
1929-08-24;217(2):404.

Sprigge S, Morland E eds.. Dietary Principles in tuberculosis. Lancet
1929-09-21;217(2):617.

Sprigge S, Morland E eds.. Dietetic therapeutics of Tuberculosis of the
Skin. Lancet 1930-08-09;219(2):311

Sprigge S, Morland E eds.. Dietetic Treatment of Tuberculosis of the
Skin. Lancet 1931-03-14;220(1):610

Sprigge S, Morland E eds.. The Gerson Diet for Dermatoses. Lancet
1931-05-30;220(1):1201

Sprigge S, Morland E eds.. The Gerson Diet. Lancet 1931-06-20;220(1):
1366-1367

Sprigge S, Morland E eds.. The Gerson diet. Lancet 1932-03-19;222(1):
629

Sprigge S, Morland E eds.. The diet of Gerson. Lancet
1932-03-26;222(1):708

Starcke H. [Erfahrung mit der salzlosen diat nach Gerson und hermannsdorfer bei Kindern und Jungendlichen.] Beitr. z. Klin. d. Tuberk. 1930;74:61-88

Stein H. [Erfahrung mit Diatkuren bei der Lungentuberkulost.] Ztschr. f. Tuberk. 1930;58(6):426-431

Strauss H. [Diat als Heilfactor.] Med Welt 1930-02-08;4(6):171-175

Stub-Christensen. Dietetics and Tuberculosis, with Especial Regard to Calcium Metabolism and to Significance of vitamins. Hospitalsitdende, Copenhagen 1931-02-05;74:157

Stumpf R. Case of lupus vulris treated by roentgen therapy and Gerson diet. Ir J Med Sci 1930-06;:254-257

Stumpke G, Mohrmann BHU. Dietary Therapy of Lupus and Other Skin Diseases. Med Klin 1931-02-13;27:235

Sylla A, Schone G. [Zur Ernahrungsbehandlung der Lungentuberkulose nach Sauerbruch-Herrmanns-dorfer-Gerson (S.H.G.).] Beitr. z. Klin. d. Tuberk. 1931;78:678-696

Symposium. [DieBedeutung der von Sauerbruch, Herrmannsdorfer und Gerson angegebenen Diat bei der Behandlung der Tuberkulose.] Veroffentl. a. d. Geb. d. Med.-Verwalt. 1930;32:541-632

Szold E. Treatment of tuberculosis of the urinary tract with the Sauerbruch-herrmannsdorfer-Gerson diet. Orv Hetil 1931-11-21;75:1130-1132

Tesdal M. [DieDiat von Gerson-Herrmannsdorfer-Sauerbruch und deren Einwirkung auf den Stoffwechsel.] Z Klin Med 1932;121:184-193

Tesdal M. Effect of Gerson-herrmannsdorfer-Sauerbruch diet on metabolism in tuberculosis. Norsk. mag. f. laegevidensk 1932-10;93:1073-1082

Timpano P. [Ladietoterapia e la radiumterapia del lupus vulgaris.] rinasc. med 1933-04-15;10:184-185

Traub EF. A case for diagnosis (Tuberculosis). Arch. Dermat. Syph. 1934;30:592-593

Appendix F

Unverricht. The Influence of an Unsalted Diet upon the Gastric Secretion, and the clinical Use of Such Diet. Dtsch Med Wochenschr 1933-08;

Urbach E, Lewinn EB. Skin Disease, Nutrition, and Metabolism, Chapter XIX: cutaneous Tuberculosis, pgs. 530-537. New York, Grune & Stratton, 1946 (orig 1932).

Urbach E. Skin Diseases and Nutrition, including the Dermatoses of children (trans. F.R. Schmidt). Vienna: Wilhelm Maudrich, 1932.

Urbach E, LeWinn EB. [?] ;
Valagussa F. [Lacura dietetica della tuberculosi medianti il metodo Gerson-herrmannsdorfer-Sauerbruch.] Bull.e. atti. D. R. Acad .med. di Roma 1930-01;56:15-24

Van Kampen F. [DeGerson-Therapie.] Nederlands Tijdschrift voor Integrale Geneeskunde 1985;8:53-57

Van Kampen F. [Detheorie van de Gersonbehandeling.] Nederlands Tijdschrift voor Integrale Geneeskunde 1985;10:199-204

Varela B, Recarte P, Esculies J. [Sauerbasengleich und ionisiertes kalzium im Blute der Tuberkulosen und ihre

Veranderungen bei Minarldiatterapie nach Sauerbruch-Herrmannsdorfer-Gerson.] Atschr. f. Tuberk. 1930;57(6):380-390

Vaucher E, Grunwald E. [LeTraitement dietetique do la tuberculose pulmonaire, Revue critique sur les travaux de G-S-H.] Paris med. 1930-01;1:25-30

Volk R. [Therapie des Lupus vulgaris und die Gerson-Diat.] Wien Klin Wochenschr 1930-11-27;43(48):1461-1466

Volk R. [Zur Diattherapie von Hautkrankheiten.] Dermatol Wochenschr 1931-12-20;91(51):1869-1873

Volk R. [Ladieta sin sal segun Sauerbruch-Herrmannsdorfer-Gerson en la tuberculosis extrapulmonar.] Rev. mex. de. tuberc. 1940-01/02;2:5-23

Ward PS. History of the Gerson therapy. Contract report prepared for the U.S. Office of Technology Assessment. U.S. Government Printing Office, 1988

Waterhouse C, Terepka AR. Metabolic observations during the forced feeding of patients with cancer Am Jour Med 1956-02;:

Waterhouse C, Craig A. Body-composition and changes in patients with advanced cancer Cancer 1957-11/12;11(6):

Watson C. Gerson Diet for Tuberculosis. Lancet 1930-07-19;218(2):161

Watson C. Gerson Treatment of Tuberculosis. Br Med J 1930-08-23;2:284-285

Watson C. Diet and nutrition with special reference to the Sauerbruch-Herrmannsdorfer-Gerson diet. Med. Press. 1930-09-10;130:207-209

Watson C. The Vital Factor in Diet: A Theory of the Nature of Vitamins. Edinburgh. Med. J. 1931-01/12;38:91-104

Watson C. The Vital Factor in Diet. Nature 1931-07-25;3221(128):154

Watson C. The Gerson Regime in Pulmonary Tuberculosis: With a Note on the Radiological Findings by Dr. J.S. Fulton. Trans. Med.-Chir. Soc. Edinburgh 1932-11-02;:6-20

Weise O. [Erfahrungen mit der "Diatebehandlung nach Gerson-Herrmannsdorfer-Sauerbruch" bei verschiednen Tuberkulose formen des Kindesalters.] Ztschr. f. Kinderh 1931-05;51:119-126

Weisl N von. [Einiges uber die praktische Durchfuhrung der Gerson-Diat.] Fortschr Med 1935-03-11;53:185-188

Welsch MA, Cohen LA, Welsch CW. Inhibition of growth of human breast carcinoma xenografts by energy expenditure via voluntary exercise in athymic mice fed a high-fat diet. Nutr Cancer 1995;23(3):309-317

White CJ. Lupus Vulgaris (Treated by the Gerson Diet). Lupus Erythematosus? Archiv. Dermat. Syph. 1931;24:323-324

White CJ. Tuberculosis of the Skin. IMJ Ill Med J 1931-07/12;60:215-218

Wichmann P. [Uber die Beeinflussung der Hauttuberkulose durch die Diat nach Gerson.] Beitr. z. Klin. d. Tuberk. 1928;66:464

Appendix F

Wichmann P. [Ergebnisse der Diatbehandlung der Hauttuberkulose.] Klin Wochenschr 1929-12-17;8(51):2366-2368.

Wichmann P. [Verschlimmerung von Haut-und Schleimhauttuberkulose durch Gerson-Diat.] Beitr. a. Klin. d. Tuberk. 1930;73:825-828

Wichmann P. [Ergebnisse der Gerson-Sauerbruch-Herrmannsdorfer-Diat-Behandlung bei Haut- und Schleim-hauttuberkulose.] Beitr. a. Klin. d. Tuberk. 1930;75:100-103

Wichmann P. Reply to Gerson. Klin Wochenschr 1930-04-12;9:694

Wohlfarth. [Erfahrungen mit HGS-Diat bei Lungentuberkulose.] Ztschr. g. artzl. Fortbild 1932-09-15;29(18):559-563

Wolff-Eisner A. [DieGerson Sauerbruch Tuberkulose-Diat im Urteil der Fachkritik.] Beitr. z. Klin. d. Tuberk. 1929;73:829-834.

Zelinka J. Gerson-Herrmannsdorfer-Sauerbruch diet in therapy of osseous tuberculosis. Cas Lek Cesk 1932-03-18;71(12):357-

Zelinka J. Gerson-Herrmannsdorfer-Sauerbruch diet in therapy of osseous tuberculosis. Cas Lek Cesk 1932-03-25;71(13):391-395

Ziegler O. [DieGrunde der Ablehnung der salzlosen Dieat durch die Tuberkuloseheilanstalten.] Dtsch Med Wochenschr 1931-01-02;57:11-13

Appendix G

Vegan/Holistic Arizona Businesses

Naturopathic Medicine and Homeopathy
Ben Ta'ati CCH, RSHom - Homeopath
Dr. Judith Jones - Family Physician
Dr. Amalia Baca - Family Physician
Dr. Carrie Rittling - Pediatrician

MDs
Dr. Deborah Dykema - Family Physician
Dr. Christopher Bressler - Family Physician

GYN
Dr. Deborah Wilson

Fitness/Personal Trainers
Ryan Furman - Mainly Plants
Will Tucker - Will Tucker Fitness
Vaness Espinoza - Plant Based Muscle

Small Business
Lisa: The Eyebrow Queen
Organic Skin By Myriam
Wild Clover Botanicals
Rocco's Sweet Shoppe
Mindful Youth Project
The Wild Rabbit Raw
Aloha Yoga and Hula
Plant Powered Prep
So Original Beads
Souls Unfolding
La PupuSarita
Zen Comfort

About the Author

Elizabeth Joseph has been a foodie her whole life. Spending 14 years in the restaurant industry, her love for food blossomed into a career in the kitchen. As she began to learn the truth about our food industry and health, she was determined to change her life. She engulfed herself in the natural healing world and attended summits, seminars, retreats, and lectures learning as much as she could from the nation's top doctors, researchers and pioneers in the natural health world.

After 10 years of drinking and eating her way through fast food, drugs and alcohol, she turned a new leaf. Elizabeth decided to make a business following her passions. *Be More Raw* makes satisfying, delicious and medicinal food. She teaches families how to heal themselves with nourishing food, essential oils and herbs.

Be More Raw helps individuals taper off from or eliminate their medication usage. She works with multiple doctors around the valley. She has helped clients find relief from diseases including cancer, diabetes, and GI issues as well as helping individuals who simply want to make better food decisions.

www.bemoreraw.com